Gender and Sexual Diversity in Schools

EXPLORATIONS OF EDUCATIONAL PURPOSE

Volume 10

Series Scope

In today's dominant modes of pedagogy, questions about issues of race, class, gender, sexuality, colonialism, religion, and other social dynamics are rarely asked. Questions about the social spaces where pedagogy takes place – in schools, media, and corporate think tanks – are not raised. And they need to be.

The *Explorations of Educational Purpose* book series can help establish a renewed interest in such questions and their centrality in the larger study of education and the preparation of teachers and other educational professionals. The editors of this series feel that education matters and that the world is in need of a rethinking of education and educational purpose.

Coming from a critical pedagogical orientation, *Explorations of Educational Purpose* aims to have the study of education transcend the trivialization that often degrades it. Rather than be content with the frivolous, scholarly lax forms of teacher education and weak teaching prevailing in the world today, we should work towards education that truly takes the unattained potential of human beings as its starting point. The series will present studies of all dimensions of education and offer alternatives. The ultimate aim of the series is to create new possibilities for people around the world who suffer under the current design of socio-political and educational institutions.

For further volumes:
http://www.springer.com/series/7472

Elizabeth J. Meyer

Gender and Sexual Diversity in Schools

An Introduction

 Springer

Prof. Elizabeth J. Meyer
Concordia University
Dept. of Education
1455 de Maissonneuve Blvd. W., LB 581
Montreal, QC H3G 1M8
Canada
emeyer@education.concordia.ca

ISBN 978-94-007-0487-9   ISBN 978-90-481-8559-7   (eBook)
DOI 10.1007/978-90-481-8559-7
Springer Dordrecht Heidelberg London New York

Library of Congress Control Number: 2010923083

Springer is part of Springer Science+Business Media (www.springer.com)

For mom and dad
Thank you for your boundless love and support.
I am humbled and awed by your desire to keep
learning and to help make the world a better
place. I love you.

Acknowledgments

I must start by extending my deepest gratitude to the late Joe Kincheloe who encouraged me to write this text. His guidance, vision, and support made this book possible. Shirley Steinberg has also been an unbelievable mentor to me and an important advocate for work in gender and sexual diversity studies, and I am thankful for her strength, endurance, and love through this very difficult year. This text was made immeasurably better from the comments of "critical friends" who took the time to read chapters, to ask questions, to provide valuable suggestions, and to offer detailed feedback. A deep thanks goes to Veronika Lesiuk, Erica Meiners, Gerald Walton, Connie North, Janna Jackson, and Liz Airton. Also, big thanks to my editor at Springer, Harmen van Paradijs whose patience and guidance allowed me to take the time I needed to get this book right.

I also want to recognize the students in my Introduction to Sexual Diversity Studies course (Fall 2008) at McGill University who read several chapters and through their questions and discussion enabled me to improve those sections. I really enjoyed teaching this course and was impressed and inspired by the deep level of engagement, respect, and care most students brought to this course. Teaching this class was an amazing opportunity and I believe that my experiences developing the course material and engaging with students in deep conversations around these ideas helped me make this a text that will be more useful to others who integrate this content into their own courses.

My work in this field has been strengthened and pushed by my colleagues in the American Educational Research Association's Queer Studies Special Interest Group. It is through discussions, conference sessions, publications, and events with these scholars that I have been pushed to extend my knowledge and understanding of gender and sexual diversity issues. This subject matter is marginalized in most educational institutions – particularly in schools of education, therefore these relationships were vital to my development as a scholar in this field. I want to particularly mention Catherine Lugg and Wayne Martino whose mentorship and leadership in this field have been incredibly valuable to me.

I would also like to take this opportunity to acknowledge several community and educational groups whose work has provided important resources and information for me and other educators and researchers engaged in work around sexual and gender diversity issues: The Gay, Lesbian, and Straight Education Network

(GLSEN) – particularly their fantastic research department including Joe Kosciw, Emily Greytak, and Elizabeth Diaz; Groundspark, who produces incredible educational films; EGALE Canada's Education Committee; and the California Safe Schools Coalition. These groups, along with the local organizations and initiatives that they support, have been instrumental in helping to make schools safer and more inclusive for all students and community members.

It is important to acknowledge you, the reader, and the countless other educators and community advocates who are interested in learning more about gender and sexual diversity in schools and taking action to make them more inclusive and welcoming learning environments for all students. Thank you for investing the time and the energy in this important work. I hope you will take the ideas and suggestions in this text and find ways to adapt them to your unique settings to assist you in all of your efforts to work towards social justice and equity.

Finally I would like to thank my wife, Veronika Lesiuk, for her continued love and support. Her interest in my career projects as well as her editing and critical thinking skills have been an incredible gift. I am so grateful to have a partner who is so committed to helping everything I do be the best it can be.

Contents

Part I
Understanding Gender
and Sexual Diversity

Chapter 1
Introduction: Why Learn About Gender and Sexual Diversity in Schools?

Myths and misconceptions about sexual and gender diversity:

(1) When talking about sexual or gender diversity, it really just means teaching about homosexuality.
(2) Learning about gender and sexuality isn't relevant for education professionals and youth workers – particularly those in elementary education.
(3) Teaching about gender and sexual diversity is controversial and should be avoided in schools.
(4) Some religions teach that homosexuality is wrong, so schools shouldn't talk about sexual diversity as it may violate some students' religious or cultural beliefs.

1.1 Introduction

Issues relating to gender and sexual diversity have always been present in schools. Many aspects of school life are constructed around traditional sex roles: girls and boys would enter the school building from separate doors, girls studied home economics and boys went to wood shop. Teachers were unmarried women and principals and superintendents were men (Blount, 1996, 2005). Although in the twenty-first century many of these traditions have become less rigid, the lasting impacts of these practices are still felt today.

Schools play a key role in teaching and reinforcing the dominant values of culture and this holds especially true in areas of gender and sexuality. From the first day they enter pre-school or kindergarten, children are identified by their sex on registration forms, referred to as "boys and girls," and their gender is consistently practiced and reinforced through stories, free play, and interactions with their teachers and their peers (Blaise, 2005; Renold, 2000). Schools are also a popular site for exploring exclusive relationships with "best friends" in primary school and "boyfriends" or "girlfriends" in the later years (Renold, 2003, 2006). It is often where youth develop their first crushes and learn about families, relationships, reproduction, and what society expects them to be. So much of what occurs in school is gendered or sexualized and for this reason it is important that educators have a strong understanding of how systems of sex, gender, and sexuality operate in the K–12 setting.

E.J. Meyer, *Gender and Sexual Diversity in Schools*, Explorations of Educational Purpose 10, DOI 10.1007/978-90-481-8559-7_1, © Springer Science+Business Media B.V. 2010

This book is designed to provide future teachers and administrators, as well as other school professionals and youth workers, a better understanding of how the interrelated systems of gender and sexuality impact students' experiences in school. For many students this is a matter of life or death: students who have acted out violently against others or themselves have often been described as being outcasts in school because they weren't masculine enough, or had been perceived to be gay or lesbian (Kellner, 2009; Kimmel & Mahler, 2003; Klein, 2006; Phillips, 2007; Stoudt, 2006). The 1999 Columbine massacre in Colorado, the 2008 school shooting of Lawrence King in California (Abdollah, 2008; Kellner, 2009; Setoodeh, 2008), and the 2009 suicide of 11-year-old Carl Walker-Hoover (McGuiness, 2009) are just three highly publicized examples of this phenomenon.

This chapter outlines many of the pressing issues that are implicated in discussions of sex, gender, and sexuality in schools. The first section introduces five key areas that can have a significant influence on students' experiences in schools. The second section gives examples from the curriculum, extracurricular activities, and school structures to show how sexual and gender diversity are already present in schools, but generally aren't addressed in positive or inclusive ways. The final section provides an overview of seven philosophies of education and how each of these approaches explicitly argues for a more thorough discussion of issues relating to gender and sexuality in schools.

1.2 Why Understand Gender and Sexual Diversity in Schools?

I have taught about issues related to gender and sexual diversity in schools for the past 15 years and am used to experiencing resistance from students, parents, and professional educators on the topic. It is common for students to resist discussing topics that make them uncomfortable or for which they have no previous experiences in schools. When introducing topics related to gender and sexual diversity it is important to acknowledge that students in the class or workshop attendees will be in very different places with regards to their knowledge of and comfort with gender and sexual diversity issues. In order to create a positive learning environment and allow each student to engage meaningfully with these ideas, this book aims to offer an accessible introduction to several compelling reasons why it is important for educators to become knowledgeable about these issues. This first section addresses four areas: student safety, physical and emotional health, diversity and equity, and student engagement and success.

1.2.1 Student Safety

Student safety is one of the most pressing reasons to explicitly address issues of gender and sexual diversity in schools. Bullying and harassment are prevalent in schools and peak in early elementary and again when students hit puberty around age 11–14

(Craig, in preparation). Much of this bullying and harassment is gendered ir it isolates and targets individuals who don't conform to dominant notions o sexual masculinity and femininity (Dijkstra, Lindenberg, & Veenstra, 2007; Meyer, 2006, 2009). Boys who are sensitive or not athletic and girls who enjoy physical activities or aren't considered attractive are popular targets. Anti-gay name-calling and jokes are also common in schools (Kosciw, Diaz, & Gretytak, 2008). This intolerance among youth for gender non-conformity and their learned homophobia needs to be addressed. Students who are targeted for this form of harassment are at high risk for drug abuse, dropping out, and suicide (California Safe Schools Coalition, 2004). Students who are bisexual, gay, lesbian, queer, questioning their sexuality or transgender (BGLQT[1]) or have BGLQT family members learn to feel afraid and ashamed in school because these homophobic and transphobic behaviors are tolerated and even perpetuated by school personnel (Kosciw & Diaz, 2008; Meyer, 2009). Educators need to learn the language and the skills to interrupt gendered harassment at all ages so youth learn that these forms of bias are not acceptable.

1.2.2 Physical and Emotional Health

A second reason that educators must improve their understandings of gender and sexual diversity in schools is to improve the physical and emotional health of all youth. As noted above, many students feel ostracized and isolated in schools and this has long-term negative impacts on their physical and emotional well-being (Graham & Bellmore, 2007; Gruber & Fineran, 2007; Rigby & Slee, 1999; Slee, 1995; R. Young & Sweeting, 2004). In addition to the threats of physical and sexual assault, many youths try to escape these hostile environments through unhealthy behaviors such as skipping or quitting school, drug and alcohol abuse, high-risk sexual behaviors, and even suicide (Kosciw et al., 2008; *Massachusetts High School Students and Sexual Orientation: Results of the 1999 Youth Risk Behavior Survey*, 1999; van Wormer & McKinney, 2003).

1.2.3 Diversity and Equity

Schools are also designed to prepare students to become active and engaged citizens in a democratic society. In order to meet the needs of all students, schools have slowly begun to adapt to include the voices, perspectives, and experiences of all members of our multicultural society. Issues of diversity and equity are of prime

---

[1]I am using the abbreviation BGLQT in this book, however you may also see written as GLBT, LGBT, or GLB. I have chosen to list the letters in alphabetical order since many groups feel that the order of the letters may indicate a priority being placed on the issues of gay men and/or lesbians. In the spirit of equality, I have opted to use alphabetical order: BGLQT. In other parts of this volume, you may see only LGB which indicates that transgender people or the term "queer" were not addressed in that particular study or publication.

importance to address in order to ensure that all children have an equal opportunity of success in school. Although many schools have made progress in diversifying their curricula and school activities to recognize and include people of diverse religious, linguistic, ethnic, and racial backgrounds, much work still needs to be done. In addition to improving our efforts at making schools more inclusive of diverse students and their families in these areas, we need to begin to specifically address issues of gender identity and expression and sexual diversity as well. If we hope to live in a society that values all people and where every child has an opportunity at success, then we need to continue finding ways to teach inclusively about the hidden and marginalized experiences as well as the dominant and mainstream perspectives.

1.2.4 Student Engagement and Academic Success

The fourth reason it is important to begin addressing gender and sexual diversity in schools is to create positive school climates to improve student engagement and academic success. School climate is a term used to describe the environment or culture of a learning community. In order to create a learning environment that is inclusive and supportive of all students in a school community, it is important to include information about gender and sexual diversity along with other multicultural education initiatives. In Massachusetts, they have implemented the only statewide program to improve school safety for gay and lesbian youth, the Safe Schools Program for Gay and Lesbian Youth (SSP). The SSP mandates schools to take four key steps to improve their school climates by (1) developing school policies protecting gay and lesbian students from harassment, violence, and discrimination, (2) offering training to school personnel in crisis and suicide intervention, (3) supporting the establishment of school-based support groups for gay, lesbian, and heterosexual students (Gay-Straight Alliances), and (4) providing school-based counseling for family members of gay and lesbian students (Perrotti & Westheimer, 2001). In one evaluation of this program, researchers found that students in schools that implemented at least one element of the SSP believe that "their school is a safer, less sexually prejudiced environment than those in schools without any aspect of the SSP" (Szlacha, 2003, p. 73). Although it is essential to ensure students' basic physical safety in schools, educators must take steps to move beyond merely removing physical harms to actively creating a positive school climate where every student feels welcome and accepted so that they can learn.

Finally, in order to maximize students' opportunities for academic success, we have to teach about gender and sexual diversity in the curriculum. By improving the diversity climate of a school, through policy updates and diversifying the curriculum, harassment and other biased behaviors can be reduced. In one study, students reported less harassment and stronger feelings of school safety when teachers stopped name-calling (California Safe Schools Coalition, 2004). Recent research indicates that students who are harassed in school for being BGLT are more likely to miss school and less likely pursue higher education (Kosciw et al., 2008, p. 85;

Russell et al., 2006). Therefore, if we reduce these barriers it is logical to conclude that fewer students would miss school, and more would continue on to higher education. Additionally, students who report experiencing less harassment based on sexual orientation or gender identity and expression have higher GPAs and are more likely to graduate and pursue higher education than BGLT students who report experiencing more repeated and severe harassment in school (Kosciw et al., 2008, p. 86).

1.3 Issues in Schools

Issues of gender and sexual diversity are prevalent throughout K–12 schools. Most aspects of school life can fall into one of three broad categories: curriculum, extracurricular activities, and school climate. Each of these three areas of school life has gender and sexuality issues already present. Unfortunately, without explicit awareness and teaching about gender and sexual diversity, there are often myths and misconceptions that get perpetuated in these areas that allow hostile and negative attitudes toward BGLQT people and their family members to grow and persist. Chapters 4 and 7 address these issues in greater depth, but I introduce some basic information here to provide the reader with a general understanding of how gender and sexual diversity issues are already present in schools.

1.3.1 Curriculum

When speaking about the curriculum, this book addresses the core content and learning objectives that are formally part of a school's mandate. This includes lessons, texts, films, field trips, visiting speakers and assemblies, library materials, and other learning activities that are part of the official state or provincial curricular programs. Gender and sexuality are already quite prevalent in the school curriculum. In elementary schools children are often asked to speak about their families and to write stories, draw pictures, and relate lessons to their own home life. When speaking about families and home lives the topic of parents and other important caregivers is central. Due to the fact that many children live in homes that have different family arrangements than a heterosexual nuclear family, issues of sexual and family diversity are already present in most schools. Additionally, children are taught to explore various interests and experiences through creative play and other experiential activities in elementary school. Many of these games and activities are loaded with gender codes, such as the dress-up corner, building blocks and trucks, mini-kitchen sets, and even books in bins sorted by "boys' interests" and "girls' interests." Children work very hard to learn to understand categories, and the rules of gender are some of the most powerful categories that children struggle to understand. It is for these reasons that elementary teachers must be aware of issues relating to gender and sexual diversity in their classrooms.

In secondary schools, the language arts curriculum is full of novels, plays, and poems of heterosexual romantic love, science and health lessons on reproduction, and historical examples of sex roles in society. Math classes often have tacit messages embedded in word problems and the information in charts and graphs often use sex as a category to organize and quantify information. In order to offer students a different way of understanding these materials, we must include information about gender and sexual diversity so they can think critically about these lessons and texts and not blindly reproduce old stereotypes and misinformation that has been embedded through the repetition of these lessons. Chapter 4 addresses this topic in greater detail.

1.3.2 Extracurricular Activities

Extracurricular activities include all other activities that are somehow supported by the school but students are not obligated to attend. Common examples of these activities include student government, sports teams, drama club, speech/debate teams, and special interest groups such as the young Republicans, ethno-cultural groups, 4-H, Bible study, and Gay–Straight Alliances. Most traditional extracurricular activities have subtexts that subtly and overtly teach that certain forms of masculinity and femininity are valued over others. The clearest example of such an activity is that of competitive athletics teams and the cheerleaders and dance squads that accompany them. In general, it is the male athletes who are praised for their speed, strength, aggressiveness, and ability to win, and the female performers who are appreciated for their grace, agility, physical beauty, and ability to entertain (Adams & Bettis, 2008). Other extracurricular activities that reinforce these stereotypes include fundraisers for clubs that include flowers or candy exchanges around Valentine's Day, Halloween dances, and the prom. There are other clubs and activities where the messages about gender and sexual diversity are less overt such as chess club, math club, chorus, and orchestra. Often young men who participate in such groups are targets for jokes regarding their masculinity and sexuality. There are also other spaces where there are already many opportunities to explore gender and sexual diversity such as the drama club and Gay–Straight Alliances or other diversity-themed groups. These are discussed at greater length in Chapter 4. In addition to understanding how gender and sexual diversity are already present in the curriculum and extracurricular activities, it is important to recognize how these issues also permeate the culture of a school.

1.3.3 School Climate

As mentioned earlier, creating a positive school climate is an important goal in order to create the conditions that will encourage the most students to succeed and thrive in school. Unfortunately, many school climates are hostile and toxic for many students. The climate of a school is created by the interaction of many formal and informal factors (Meyer, 2008). Some of the formal factors that influence the climate of the school include physical plant, official policies and mission statements, school administrators, the professional staff, and the formal curriculum. Informal factors interact with the formal ones and have a powerful influence on the overall climate experienced by students and staff at the school. Some of the informal factors include administrators' leadership style, educational philosophies and relationships among professional staff, youth cultures, and the dominant values of the school community. Every school community has elements of diversity in it, however, the level to which it embraces and recognizes this diversity as valuable or negligible is important.

Unfortunately, many school cultures are extremely hostile toward any form of gender and sexual diversity: they overtly send messages that students and their families who do not conform to the heterosexual gender norms of that community are not welcome and may be subject to both psychological and physical violence. Other schools are not overtly toxic. However the silencing and marginalization of gender and sexual diversity issues also tell community members that they are not valued or welcome to be fully themselves at school. Finally, some schools have made concerted efforts to actively discuss and teach about gender and sexual diversity. These schools may have professional staff who are bisexual, gay, lesbian, queer, or transgender people and students or parents who are active and involved who are publicly known to be BGLQT. Chapters 6 and 7 address the issues of school climate in greater detail. In order to better understand how issues of gender and sexual diversity connect with current philosophies of education, the next section presents an introduction to several important educational theories and how these approaches to understanding education advocate for greater inclusion of gender and sexual diversity issues in schools.

1.4   Theoretical Foundations

A central feature of most pre-service teacher education programs is for future teachers to reflect on and develop their own philosophy of teaching. This exercise is important in order for educators to have a strong theoretical foundation for the choices that they make in the classroom and to offer them the opportunity to ground their personal beliefs about education in the current knowledge and research that we have about teaching and learning. If one has a cohesive and clearly formulated teaching philosophy, then a teacher can create more intentional and well-grounded learning experiences for one's students as well as make snap decisions about how to respond in certain situations. This section provides an introduction to seven main schools of educational thought and demonstrates how each one advocates for the inclusion of gender and sexual diversity. The seven theories are democratic, critical pedagogy, feminist, social justice, multicultural, anti-oppressive, and queer.

1.4.1 Democratic Theories of Education

Democracy and education have been linked as far back as Ancient Greece in the writings of Aristotle (384–322 bc.) (Fraser, 1996, p. 139). Democratic theories of education have been central to the institution of public schooling in the United States and Canada since the inception of free, compulsory, public education. Horace Mann (1796–1859), W.E.B. DuBois (1868–1963) and John Dewey (1859–1952), were early advocates for public education in the United States. More recent scholars have built on the early writings of these important thinkers to push the notions of democratic education and equal educational opportunity. In his book, *Understanding equal educational opportunity: Social justice and democracy in schooling*, Howe (1997) expands on the thesis presented by Amy Gutmann (1987) in her book, *Democratic education*. Gutmann's central idea is as follows:

> A democratic theory of education recognizes the importance of empowering citizens to make educational policy and also of constraining their choices among policies in accordance with those principles – of nonrepression and nondiscrimination – that preserve the intellectual and social foundations of democratic deliberations. A society that empowers citizens to make educational policy, moderated by these two principled constraints, realizes the democratic ideal of education (Gutman, 1987, p. 14).

Gutmann (1987) states that the principle of non-repression prevents any group from "using education to restrict rational deliberation of competing conceptions of the good life and the good society," and that non-discrimination can be understood as "a principle of non-exclusion" (pp. 44–45). However, Howe charges that Gutmann's "general principle of 'non-repression' (of which 'nondiscrimination' is a derivative) is too weak to adequately protect marginalized and oppressed groups in negotiating the participatory ideal" (1997, p. 66). Nonoppression is offered in its place, for Howe believes that a "stronger principle – a principle of nonoppression – is required in order to protect groups that are threatened with marginalization and exclusion from meaningful democratic participation" (1997, p. 67).

Nonoppression is a more powerful concept than Gutman's non-repression. There are many non-discrimination policies in schools, businesses, and government designed to protect minorities from unjust exclusion. These policies make it illegal to refuse admission or hiring to people based on race, gender, religion, and other factors. If a business or a school is forced to admit a woman or a person of color due to these policies, it is likely that the work climate will not be conducive to the success of that minority member. Incidents that display covert racism (e.g., not inviting the new worker to join "the gang" for lunch, or extremely close supervision and monitoring of work) and sexual harassment (e.g., telling a woman that she has "great legs" and should wear skirts more often, or referring the female employees as "babe" or "honey") may impede the ability of that individual to work to his/her best capability. The same holds true for students in a school setting. If the climate is not supportive of every child in the school, then true educational opportunities "worth wanting"(Howe, 1997) do not exist. It is not enough to legally remove the barriers preventing their entrance, but we must also go a step further and begin to remove the oppressive language and structures that create a hostile climate for minority students.

Howe's concept of recognition parallels Gutmann's principle of tolerance, but again is "more demanding in its requirements" (Howe, 1997, p. 68). Howe chooses recognition in place of tolerance, for he believes that tolerance is not adequate. If educators are merely tolerating, or putting up with, the diverse students in their classrooms, then these students aren't being offered a fighting chance at success, or an educational opportunity worth wanting.

There has been significant debate over how to create Equal Educational Opportunity (EEO), and whether or not it truly exists. The counter-arguments include such rhetoric as there are no legal or physical barriers preventing these populations from accessing the educational system, therefore EEO does exist. Yet Jonathan Kozol (1991), in his book *Savage inequalities*, vividly and powerfully showed how, with the absence of legal barriers, EEO still does not exist. Kozol looked specifically at economic inequalities, but the schools which were in the poorest conditions were schools with large ethnic and racial minority populations. In other words, Kozol reported that schools in inner cities that have many students of color have less funding and fewer services than schools in the suburbs that have predominantly White students.

Robert Ennis (1976), in his article, "Equality of educational opportunity," explains how students within the same school system and even the same classroom can have different kinds of opportunities. He creates a strategy for identifying what it means to "have an opportunity" by operationalizing "deterrents" and "facilitators." He identifies two factors in order to identify whether something is a deterrent. The first is determining if by eliminating a particular factor would a student be more likely to succeed. Second is to identify which factors are most likely to be responsible for the negative impacts on a student's success (p. 11).

Using Ennis' criteria, it seems evident that violence and harassment against BGLQT youth are clear deterrents to their ability to have an equal opportunity of success. For example, if a gay young man has dreams of becoming a lawyer, he must be competitive in high school in order to gain admission to a good college to prepare for law school. However, if in his high school this boy is harassed by his teachers and students in his classes, then it is logical that his academic performance would decline in the face of these obstacles. Therefore, Criterion 1 is satisfied: eliminating the harassment would have made his academic success more likely. It then follows that Criterion 2 is fulfilled: the harassment has lessened the likelihood of the student doing well in school, which reduces his chances for entry into a competitive college, which then reduces the chances of his entry into and completion of law school.

Ennis also discusses how a facilitator can augment a student's educational opportunities. Examples of facilitators include having college-educated parents, access to additional educational materials (computers, museums, etc.), and cultural values that are reinforced in schools. Many students have both facilitators and deterrents to equal opportunity. Schools can and should actively enhance facilitators as well as work to reduce deterrents for all students. To attain EEO, schools must actively attempt to counteract the deterrents that arise as a result of the school's climate and curriculum. In the case of BGLQT youth, such deterrents include violence, harassment, parental rejection, widespread homophobia leading to self-destructive behaviors, and other forms of oppression discussed throughout this book. Howe's (1997) framework of "educational opportunities worth wanting" effectively sets the tone to remove many of these deterrents, and replace them with facilitators that will offer every student opportunities worth wanting.

Equal educational opportunity theory clearly advocates for the inclusion of accurate and positive information regarding gender and sexual diversity in schools to ensure that all students have educational opportunities worth wanting. In order for BGLQT students, students of BGLQT parents, as well as gender non-conforming youth to have meaningful opportunities for success in schools, information about their lives and their families must be integrated across the curriculum. A second theory of education that shares similar goals with democratic theories of education, but has different theoretical roots, is that of critical pedagogy.

1.4.2 Critical Pedagogy

Critical theory and its applications in the field of education, critical pedagogy, is a school of thought that grew out of work developed by the Frankfurt School that included scholars such as Max Horkheimer, Theodor Adorno, and Herbert Marcuse. They were influenced by the work of German scholars like Karl Marx, Immanuel Kant, Georg Hegel, and Max Weber, but went beyond the critiques of economic oppression offered by these thinkers (Kincheloe, 2005). Although capitalism and the related class system was the primary object of critique, these theories were expanded upon and used to understand oppression, alienation, and inequality in society on many other levels. The early work of these theorists has helped many different oppressed groups understand how social forces work against them in overt and covert ways to maintain the power structures that privilege the dominant group.

Antonio Gramsci's concept of hegemony (1971/1995) is central to critical pedagogy and showed how groups in power are able to maintain structures that benefit them through gaining the consent of subordinate groups. It is not done through overt or forceful means, but rather through subtle, yet powerful, messages that repeatedly permeate daily life. He argued that "*ideology as cultural hegemony*...is an important aspect of power over society, even more than the modes of material production" (Ozmon & Craver, 1999, p. 327). In *Further selections from the prison notebooks*, Gramsci (1971/1995) wrote about education and how it contributes to hegemony: "Everything that influences or may influence public opinion directly or indirectly belongs to it: libraries, schools, groups and clubs of different kinds, right up to architecture, street lay-out and street names" (1995, p. 155). These early thinkers in the field of critical theory created the foundation upon which educational theorists could build to create the approach to education that is now called critical pedagogy.

Brazilian educator and activist Paulo Freire is widely recognized as the founder of critical pedagogy and introduced the concept of critical consciousness or *conscientização* in his famous book, *The pedagogy of the oppressed* (1970/1993). Through his work with indigenous populations in Brazil, he developed an approach to teaching and learning that was meant to empower oppressed groups to resist and counteract social structures in order to critically interrogate them and transform them. This concept of education as *praxis*, or ongoing reflective practice, was influential for many teachers and academics who shared Freire's ideals of creating a nonoppressive and equitable society.

Contemporary educational theorists such as Michael Apple, Henry Giroux, Joe Kincheloe, Madeleine Arnot, and Peter McLaren, among others, have built upon the work of these earlier theorists and examined how the explicit and hidden curricula in schools work to support existing dominant structures and contribute to the continued exclusion and oppression of marginalized groups in schools. In the preface to his book *Official knowledge*, Apple (2000) explains the core of his work as focusing on, "the struggles over meaning, space, the body, the politics of daily life in schools, the media, the state, and other sites, and the ways in which dominant groups try to maintain or restore their own meaning" (p. xviii). McLaren (1995) supports this perspective and goes further to clarify his position when he explains how certain cultural fears are reproduced in schools and serve to limit educational freedom. He explains how dynamics of race, class, gender, and sexuality are perceived and controlled in schools as ways of maintaining hegemonic dominance through the use of fear, policing, and the power of language. He addresses the importance of language and experience to identity in terms of sexuality:

> Heterosexuality has meaning only in relation to other identities such as homosexuality. That is, heterosexuality and homosexuality have no "essence" of meaning, but rather, the terms are continually and culturally negotiated within diverse historical and social arenas and in terms of competing vectors of power. Within late patriarchal capitalism, both identities have been reduced to their binary oppositions... The key imperative for critical pedagogy is to interrogate the disparity between students' everyday experiences and relations and the inherited languages of white-supremacist, homophobic, and patriarchal capitalism (pp. 112–113).

What McLaren is speaking about is the unquestioning acceptance of compulsory heterosexuality (Rich, 1978/1993) and the related gender polarization (Bem, 1993) that is repeated in schools through the official and hidden curriculum. Applying a critical pedagogy can help reduce bias and discrimination and create safer school environments for all students by making explicit gendered hierarchies in schools and exploring multiple ways of undoing and transforming the heteronormative patriarchal structures that allow them to persist.

Madeline Arnot (2002) explains, "[O]ne of the ways in which male hegemony is maintained is obviously through schooling, where it is most easy to transmit a specific set of gender definitions, relations, and differences while appearing to be objective" (2002, p. 119). She describes how gender categories are taught in schools and explains how these "arbitrary social constructs" are reproduced through various social structures such as schools, families, churches, and the media. One example of this is the role of adults in schools actively reinforcing these gender norms. It is not uncommon for students to be told to act more feminine if they are a girl, or more masculine if they are boy in order to blend in and avoid harassment and discrimination at school. One student said that when she reported harassment, "[My principal] told me to get over it. That maybe if I acted more like a girl that I wouldn't get harassed so often" (Kosciw & Diaz, 2006, p. 39). This is why it is important for all educators to understand how gender codes function and how we can work against these narrow definitions that hurt us all.

Critical pedagogy demands that teachers be emotionally and intellectually engaged in their teaching praxis and continually questioning and reexamining the "truths" and the lessons that they present to their students. Kincheloe (2005) clarifies that "teachers must become scholars who understand the multiple dimensions of the cognitive act, the reasons that it has been conceptualized so differently by different analysts at different times" (p. 131). He goes on to demand that teacher-scholars must have a deep understanding of the theoretical roots of what they are teaching in order to effectively enact a critical pedagogy in their particular set of circumstances. It is not something that can be taught in a workshop, but must be developed over a longer period of engagement with texts, competing ideas, and dialogues with self and others. This deep understanding enables teachers to be able to improvise and effectively and consistently address unanticipated teachable moments in the classroom along with prepared lessons.

Critical pedagogy requires a more diverse curriculum that includes the voices and experiences of those who have been marginalized from mainstream sources of knowledge such as state-approved textbooks, canonical literature, and mainstream media, be included in school curricula. This means that educators must work proactively and creatively to adapt their curricula to ensure that accurate and balanced information about BGLQT people, families, and culture are included in schools. Although critical pedagogy has full economic and social equality as its goal, it has often been critiqued for being dominated by White male scholars and therefore may be limited in advocating for anything other than economic equality. However, it shares many common perspectives with feminist, multicultural, and social justice theories of education. The next body of educational theory that is discussed is feminist pedagogy.

1.4.3 Feminist Pedagogy

Although Freire was widely criticized by feminists for his sexist language and assumptions in his writings pre-1980, many feminist thinkers have taken his ideas aimed at empowering exploited workers and built upon them to include anti-sexist and anti-racist work as a form of liberatory pedagogy. bell hooks explains this conflict when she wrote, "To have work that promotes one's liberation is such a powerful gift that it does not matter so much if the gift is flawed. Think of the work as water that contains some dirt. Because you are thirsty you are not too proud to extract the dirt and be nourished by the water" (1994, p. 50). hooks also points out that Freire's own concepts of critical pedagogy invites readers and activists to critically interrogate his work to point out flaws and work to address them to make the approach more meaningful and inclusive of all people. hooks proclaims,

> Feminism, as liberation struggle, must exist apart from and as a part of the larger struggle to eradicate domination in all of its forms. We must understand that patriarchal domination shares an ideological foundation with racism and other forms of group oppression, that there is no hope that it can be eradicated while these systems remain intact...This effort at revision is perhaps most evident in the current widespread acknowledgement that sexism, racism, and class exploitation constitute interlocking systems of domination – that sex, race, and class, and not sex alone, determine the nature of any female's identity, status, and circumstance, the degree to which she will or will not be dominated, the extent to which she will have the power to dominate. (hooks cited in Giroux, 1991, p. 33).

Feminist theorists have taken the work of early critical theorists and through their critique and reinterpretation of such work, have made it more effective and more inclusive of different voices and experiences in anti-oppression work

In education, feminist pedagogy has built on Freire's concepts to work toward more liberatory educational experiences for all students. In her article, *Rereading Paulo Freire*, Kathleen Weiler points out many of the similarities in the feminist and Freirean pedagogies. She explains that, "like Freirean pedagogy, feminist pedagogy emphasizes the importance of consciousness raising, the existence of an oppressive social structure and the need to change it, and the possibility of social transformation" (2001, p. 68). She goes on to make the distinction that feminist pedagogy is different in that it includes an analysis of patriarchy and attempts to develop an education that is supportive to women. In Maher and Tetreault's book, *The feminist classroom* (1994), they explain the principles shared by the feminist teachers in their study as follows: "a commitment to taking women students seriously, a consciousness of the extent to which gender is embedded in our social structures, and an understanding of the differing educational needs of different groups of students" (p. 13). They acknowledge that feminist pedagogy has much in common with other equality-based approaches to teaching and learning, however as one participant remarked, "I call myself a feminist teacher because that is the particular mode of analysis that I use to arrive at what I am trying to do" (p. 13). This is a helpful statement that can clarify the subtle distinctions among all of these related pedagogical approaches. they share common goals but are based in different disciplinary and theoretical foundations. The next related approach is multicultural education.

1.4.4 Multicultural Education

Multiculturalism, most generally, is a reform movement that seeks to equalize educational opportunities for students by diversifying the curriculum to include and teach about the contributions of individuals and cultures that are outside of the dominant Euro-centric Christian cultural frameworks in U.S. and Canadian schools. The primary "cultures" of concern that have been included under the umbrella of multiculturalism are most generally related to the categories of race, ethnicity, language, and religion. However, recently there has been a push from many theorists of multicultural education to expand this to include gender and sexual diversity as well as disability issues and inclusive education.

Theorists of multicultural education have studied multiple applications of this pedagogy and have identified various approaches that fall under the broad category of multicultural education. While these theories share an emphasis on diversity and include perspectives from various cultures and backgrounds into lessons and activities at school, there is a large divide between the impacts and theoretical foundations of these theories. James Banks (1994) has divided multicultural curriculum reform into four approaches. These include (1) the contributions approach, (2) the additive approach, (3) the social action approach, and (4) the transformation approach. Christine Sleeter and Carl Grant's work on multicultural education also provides a good overview of the field and an analysis of the variety of approaches that fall under the various interpretations and applications of multiculturalism. They divide multicultural education into five types and advocate most strongly for the fifth: "education that is multicultural and social reconstructionist" (Sleeter & Grant, 1994). Kincheloe and Steinberg (1997) similarly outline five forms of multicultural education: conservative multiculturalism/monoculturalism, liberal multiculturalism, pluralist multiculturalism, left-essentialist multiculturalism, and critical multiculturalism. Although it may seem confusing to consider these multiple understandings of multicultural education, the key point is to understand that there are widely different understandings of what multicultural education looks like and how it may change what and how knowledge is taught in school. There is not adequate space here to provide a detailed explanation of each one, so my focus here is on the approaches that most align with the goals of integrating issues of gender and sexual diversity in the curriculum.

Banks' social action approach, Sleeter and Grant's social reconstructionist approach, and Kincheloe & Steinberg's critical multiculturalism, are the ones that are most relevant to the topics and approaches to teaching advocated for in this book. These theories take the foundational principles of multicultural education and extend them to the area of greatest possible impact: critically reexamining power structures in society in order to positively transform students and society and challenge oppression and discrimination in all its forms through education. They go beyond the additive "heroes and holidays" approach to diversifying the curriculum and demand a much deeper and integrated way of teaching about diversity in schools. Although many proponents of multicultural education maintain a primary emphasis on issues of race, ethnicity, and religion, compelling arguments have been made that advocate for the inclusion of gender and sexual diversity issues in a multicultural curriculum. For example, Kincheloe and Steingberg write, "critical multiculturalism does not simply embrace issues of gender equity – though it finds them extremely important – but also rethinks the very basis of how we see the world and ourselves via the reconstructive philosophy of feminist theories" (1997, p. 137). Sleeter and Grant explain that the main objective of their social reconstructionist approach to multicultural education is, "the elimination of oppression of one gr of people by another" and they explicitly state that "this approach lends itself well to integrating concerns related to race, social class, gender, disability, and forms of oppression such as homophobia" (1994, pp. 209, 212).

Scholars have pointed to the absence of gender and sexual diversity from courses in pre-service teacher education (Britzman & Gilbert, 2004; Kissen, 2002; Letts, 2002) and teacher education texts (Macgillivray & Jennings, 2008; A. J. Young & Middleton, 2002). However, there is an emerging body of scholarship that provides texts, guidance, and models for integrating topics of gender and sexual diversity in courses and approaches to multicultural education (Meyer, 2009; Steinberg, 2009; Weis & Fine, 2005). Will Letts (2002) effectively critiques the ongoing absence of discussion of gender and sexual diversity in conversations about multicultural education and advocates for the "queering" of this pedagogical approach. He identifies the problem of nominal inclusion wherein BGLQT is added to a "laundry list" of diverse identity categories but is never "discussed in enough detail to give the reader a sense of the scope of these issues and their relevance to both multicultural-ism and teacher education" (p. 121). He explains the importance of understanding identities and cultures as dynamic and multiple and discussions of diversity and mul-ticulturalism must avoid reducing people's identities and experiences to fixed and oversimplified categories. He advocates for a critical reflexive approach to multicul-tural education that will allow a more complex and rich understanding of identities and difference to emerge. This analysis of multicultural education leads us to our discussion of social justice education which emerged in response to some of the non-critical forms of multicultural education that were being applied in many schools across the United States and Canada.

1.4.5 Social Justice

Social justice educators have many theoretical overlaps with democratic, critical, feminist, and multicultural educators. In one of the leading books on social jus-tice education, *Teaching for diversity and social justice*, Lee Anne Bell (1997) introduces the primary goals of social justice education as follows:

> The goal of social justice education is the full and equal participation of all groups in a society that is mutually shaped to meet their needs. Social justice includes a vision of soci-ety in which the distribution of resources is equitable and all members are physically and psychologically safe and secure…Social justice involves social actors who have a sense of their own agency as well as a sense of social responsibility toward and with others and the society as a whole (p. 3).

Social justice theories of education advocate for a more equal distribution of wealth and social services. In addition to economic and institutional reform, it seeks not just financial but also social equality for historically marginalized and oppressed social groups such as women, people of color, people with disabilities, and BGLQT people. Social justice approaches are closely linked to democratic theories of education and the principles of feminist and critical pedagogies mentioned earlier, but what distinguishes social justice theories of education is the explicit attention to the redistribution of social goods and services and the objective to unlearn cultural biases that privilege dominant groups and perspectives (White, middle-class, heterosexual, able-bodied, Christian, male) in existing educational structures (North, 2006). Maxine Greene (1998) explains:

> To teach for social justice is to teach for enhanced perception and imaginative explorations, for the recognition of social wrongs, of sufferings, of pestilences wherever and whenever they arise. It is to find models in literature and in history of the indignant ones, the ones forever ill at ease, and the loving ones who have taken the side of the victims of pestilences, whatever their names or places of origin. It is to teach so that the young may be awakened to the joy of working for transformation in the smallest places, so that they may become healers and change their worlds. (p. xlv)

This approach to teaching and learning may be more widely used and understood than critical pedagogy since the terminology clearly identifies the objectives of this school of thought. It focuses on repairing social wrongs for the good of the community or society as a whole. Social justice education still may be viewed as somewhat controversial at times as it can encourage students to challenge and question existing institutional practices and taken-for-granted social assumptions. It may ask them to interrogate the official stance of their school or their religion and research and reexamine deeply held values in their families or cultures. As with critical pedagogy, social justice education is generally student-centered and project-based as it seeks to engage students in dialogue, critical thinking, and a dynamic exchange of ideas and perspectives in order to give them the skills they need to be informed and active citizens who can have a positive impact on their communities (Westheimer & Kahne, 1998).

Social justice theories of education clearly advocate for the inclusion of issues related to gender and sexual diversity as a result of the systemic oppression that is experienced by students and teachers whose gender identities, expressions, and sexual orientations vary from the social scripts of masculine or feminine heterosexuality that are imbedded in the culture of schools. The perspectives, histories, and experiences of BGLQT people have been systematically excluded (Friend, 1993) from school curricula and as a result misinformation and dysconsciousness perpetuate discrimination and oppression of these individuals. Dysconsciousness is a term introduced by Joyce King (1991) specifically with regards to racism as "an uncritical habit of mind (including perceptions, attitudes, assumptions, and beliefs) that justifies inequity and exploitation by accepting the existing order of things as given" (p. 135). Dysconsciousness is a by-product of traditional forms of schooling and students engaged in a curriculum grounded in social justice would be able to actively unlearn and take active steps to address forms of it in their own homes and communities.

Henry Giroux (1998), a leading scholar in critical theory asserts, "Social justice in the curriculum must be rooted in a sense of hope, connected to the future, solidarity with others, and a willingness to fight for what one believes in. . .it can frame our work as educators only to the degree that it connects with the experiences and histories of the students we teach and work with" (p. 291). A sixth educational theory that directly supports the inclusion of issues of gender and sexual diversity in the curriculum is anti-oppressive education.

1.4.6 Anti-oppressive Education

Anti-oppressive education builds upon the earlier works of democratic, critical, and social justice educators but takes a more radical stance by explicitly naming various forms of oppression that it seeks to challenge and erase. Anti-oppressive educators link the work of anti-racist, Marxist, anti-ableist, feminist, and queer theorists. These related fields are central to understanding anti-oppressive pedagogies. In Kevin Kumashiro's (2002) work, *Troubling education: Queer activism and anti-oppressive pedagogy* he writes, "learning is about disruption and opening up to further learning, not closure and satisfaction" (p. 43) and also "education involves learning something that disrupts our commonsense view of the world" (p. 63). This concept of resistance and disruption is central to enacting an anti-oppressive pedagogy. This pedagogical approach explicitly addresses structural aspects of society that create and perpetuate various oppressions and seeks to provide students with a critical understanding of how power and privilege work in society. Educators who identify as anti-racist, anti-sexist, anti-homophobic often share similar beliefs with multicultural, critical, and feminist educators, but may be perceived to be more "radical" due to the language and approaches that they choose to employ.

Kumashiro (2002) offers four different approaches that can be used to challenge multiple forms of oppression in schools: education for the Other, education about the Other, education that is critical of privileging and Othering, and education that changes students and society (2002, p. 23). He explains that there is a time and place for each pedagogical approach, but ultimately the fourth category is the one that should guide our choices as anti-oppressive educators. In an anti-authoritarian fashion, Kumashiro explicitly states that his is not a prescriptive program, he explains:

> I do not aim to offer strategies that work. Rather, I hope to offer conceptual and cultural resources for educators and researchers to use as we rethink our practices, constantly look for new insights, and engage differently in antioppressive education...I encourage readers to think of reading this book as an event that constitutes the kind of antioppressive educational practices that I articulate throughout its discussion. It is queer in its unconventionality and it is activist in the changes it aims to bring about. In this way, my book is not a mere exercise, and not a final product, but a resource that I hope can be in some way helpful to the reader, as it was for the researcher, and as I hope it was for the participants (2002, pp. 25–26).

In this explanation he is challenging us to find our own ways of creating useful knowledge and understanding the world. He refuses to be placed in the position of "authority" where his work will be read unquestioningly and used as a one-dimensional text. Instead he is pushing educators to find new approaches to destabilize traditional ways of learning and offers different tools with which we can build that understanding. In his more recent work, *Against common sense*, he explains that, "the most significant way that anti-oppressive teaching is queer is its use of discomfort or crisis" (2004, p. 47).This is what anti-oppressive pedagogy is about. Queer pedagogy is closely linked with anti-oppressive pedagogies and will be used as an example of how anti-oppressive approaches to teaching can be applied.

1.4.7 Queer Pedagogy

Advocates of a queer pedagogy have grounded many of their assertions in critical and post-structural feminist theories. The concept of queer as a more inclusive and empowering word for the gay and lesbian experience emerged in the early 1990s as a controversial and deeply political term (Jagose, 1996, p. 76). Queer is understood as a challenge to traditional understandings of gender and sexual identity by deconstructing the categories, binaries, and language that support them. Judith Butler's *Gender trouble* (1990) and Eve Kosofky Sedgwick's *Epistemology of the closet* (1990/1993) were influential works for this emerging school of thought. Jagose explains that queer theory's most significant achievement is to specify "how gender operates as a regulatory construct that privileges heterosexuality and, furthermore, how the deconstruction of normative models of gender legitimates lesbian and gay subject-positions," (1996, p. 83). Queering seeks to disrupt and challenge traditional modes of thought around gender and sexual identity and, by standing on the boundaries or "borderlands" (Anzaldua, 1987/2007) drawn by dominant culture, can more effectively examine and dismantle them. Deborah Britzman (1995), a leading theorist in this field, explains how she understands queer theory and its role in learning:

> Queer Theory offers methods of critiques to mark the repetitions of normalcy as a structure and as a pedagogy. Whether defining normalcy as an approximation of limits and mastery, or as renunciations, as the refusal of difference itself, Queer Theory insists on posing the production of normalization as a problem of culture and of thought (p. 154).

The work of trans[2] and intersex scholars and activists have contributed to this resistance and disruption by challenging the narrow binary of sex and gender by proposing a more fluid and expansive concept of identities and expressions. Trans and intersex individuals have experienced invisibility and exclusion from gay and lesbian scholarship and activism, and queer scholars seek to address the related issues of genderism (Airton, 2009) and transphobia in their work. As individuals whose bodies and work disrupt dominant notions of sex and gender, their knowledge and experiences are influential in this study of gendered harassment in schools. Writers and activists such as Leslie Feinberg (1993, 1998), Kate Bornstein (1997), Sandra Bem (1993), Cheryl Chase (Chase, 2003), Riki Anne Wilchins (1997) and Anne Fausto-Sterling (2000) have greatly expanded our understandings of sex and

---

[2]I use the term "trans" here to refer to multiple identities that challenge the sex and gender binary: transgender, transsexual, and transformed

gender. Through their writing, performance, activism, and research, they push the boundaries of what sex and gender mean and how they are lived in different bodies. Queer theory and pedagogies have been greatly enriched and strengthened by their ideas.

Early studies of transgender individuals helped lay the foundation for reconceptualizing sex and gender in Western societies (Garfinkel 1967 cited inWest & Zimmerman, 1987, p. 131). It is the undeniability of people's lived experiences that lend credibility to much of the theoretical work of queer theory. Transgender, transsexual, and intersex individuals have experienced much harm as a result of the narrow sex and gender binaries that order patriarchal cultures. The powerful narratives offered by trans writers Feinberg, Wilchins, and Bornstein about their often painful experiences as trans people show how the sex/gender binary is flawed and does not adequately represent the full range of human experiences and identities. The scientific examination of intersex by Fausto-Sterling and the personal narrative and activism of Cheryl Chase also demonstrate how sex and gender categories are social constructs and how necessary it is that we work to transform our current understandings of them.

While marginalized groups employ new strategies to challenge dominant ideologies, these entrenched discourses push back. Resistance is offered up by the dominant structures of society to forces that try to change them. Britzman (2000) presents the queer theoretical approach to understanding this opposition in outlining three forms of resistance to sexuality: structural, pedagogical, and psychical. She defines these terms as follows: (a) structural resistance is "the very design or organization of education," (b) pedagogical resistance, "worries about Eros between students and teachers [and] considers sexuality as the secret of an individual's nature," and (c) psychical resistance as "the conflict within" (p. 34). She asserts the need to challenge all forms of resistance. She specifically addresses how sexuality is currently inserted into the school curriculum. She notes, "this has to do with how the curriculum structures modes of behaviour and orientations to knowledge that are repetitions of the underlying structure and dynamics of education: compliance, conformity, and the myth that knowledge cures" (2000, p. 35).

In discussing how to challenge *pedagogical* forms of resistance, Britzman (2000) encourages educators to recognize the power that *Eros* can play in teaching. By understanding sexuality as a force that, "allows the human its capacity for passion, interests, explorations, disappointment, and drama" and "because sexuality is both private and public – something from inside of bodies and something made between bodies – we must focus on sexuality in terms of its contradictory, discontinuous, and ambiguous workings" (2000, p. 37). Finally, in addressing *psychical* forms of resistance, Britzman advocates working through internal conflicts and ambivalence toward sexuality in order to, "raise rather serious questions on the nature of education and on the uses of educational anxiety" (p. 35). This means that educators need to explore and understand their own conflicted experiences and understandings of gender and sexuality in order to be able to facilitate and support students' explorations of these difficult topics. Potential applications of these theoretical approaches are offered in Chapter 4.

This disruption and open discussion of previously silenced issues can be a very difficult one for teachers to navigate. An anti-oppressive and queer pedagogy empowers educators to open up traditionally silenced discourses and create spaces for students to explore and challenge the hierarchy of identities that is created and supported by schools, such as teacher–student, jock–nerd, sciences–arts, male–female, black–white, rich–poor, disabled/able-bodied, and gay–straight. In order to move past this, teachers must learn to see schooling as a place to question, explore, and seek alternative explanations rather than as a place where knowledge means "certainty, authority, and stability" (Britzman, 2000, p. 51). Although the term, "queer pedagogy" might seem difficult for some teachers to embrace, it can help educators, youth advocates, schools, and other institutions creatively and effectively work to transform hostile and oppressive environments and meet the needs of all students.

1.5 Conclusion

Historically, schools have been institutions that have filled an important cultural role of teaching children to learn what has been deemed important by the people in power. In North America, these people have been overwhelmingly White, European, heterosexual, male, English-speaking, and Christian. As a result, children emerge from school having learned only the language, the history, and the ideals of this dominant culture. The recent shift toward critical pedagogy since the civil rights movement and the second-wave feminist movements of the 1960s has begun to question this type of schooling in search of a way to create students and citizens who will be critical, engaged, independent thinkers in order to move our society in a more egalitarian direction. In understanding how the forces of oppression, privilege, and social power work, educators will be better equipped to create classrooms that enact the ideals of a public education system designed to teach all students.

Queer theory offers a further application of ideas introduced by democratic education, critical pedagogy, multiculturalism as well as anti-oppressive theories, by calling on educators to question and reformulate through a queer pedagogical lens: (a) how they teach and reinforce gendered practices in schools, (b) how they support traditional notions of heterosexuality, and (c) how they present culturally specific information in the classroom. In so doing, we will be able to reduce and eventually remove all forms of discrimination from schools and consequently, most realms of society. Schools should be doing more to challenge and disrupt traditional ways of knowing and encourage students to question and "trouble" all that is normally assumed and taken for granted in society so that all students have a fair chance to learn and succeed. Institutions of learning must redefine themselves in order to move toward a truly democratic, socially just, and emancipatory learning experience. This project builds on and extends the work of critical pedagogy. Barry Kanpol (1994) explains, "the critical pedagogue always seeks just and fair ways to alter a system which, by and large, and despite seemingly good intentions, has effectively oppressed many of its members" (1994, p. 33).

By doing away with the docile, submissive, *banking* (Friere, 1970/1993) style of learning in schools, we can open up more educational possibilities and socially just experiences for future citizens rather than confine them with ideologies of traditional hegemonic, heteronormative gender roles. In order to move in this direction, it is important to understand the psychical, pedagogical, and structural resistance that prevent teachers from challenging these strict codes and police their own language and behavior in addition to that of their students.

This book is written to help current and future educators, counselors, social workers, and other youth advocates better understand how gender and sexual diversity are already present in schools as well as provide them with resources, tools, and information to create educational environments that welcome and value all forms of diversity. Please read these chapters critically and creatively and use them as a place to begin conversations, reflections, and lessons around what it might look like to teach about gender and sexual diversity in your school and your community.

References

Abdollah, T. (2008). Ventura county, hueneme school district face claims in Oxnard killing [Electronic Version]. *Los Angeles Times*. Retrieved September 7, 2008, from http://www.latimes.com/news/education/la-me-oxnard16-2008avg

Adams, N., & Bettis, P. (2008). Cheerleading. In C. Mitchell & J. Reid-Walsh (Eds.), *Girl culture: An encyclopedia* (pp. 224–226). Westport, CT: Greenwood Publishing Group.

Airton, L. (2009). Untangling 'Gender Diversity': Genderism and Its discontents (i.e., Everyone). In S. Steinberg (Ed.), *Diversity and multiculturalism: A reader* (pp. 223–245). New York: Peter Lang.

Anzaldua, G. (1987/2007). *Borderlands/La Frontera The New Mestiza*. San Francisco: Aunt Lute Books.

Apple, M. (2000). *Official knowledge: Democratic education in a conservative age* (2nd ed.). New York: Routledge.

Arnot, M. (2002). Cultural reproduction: The pedagogy of sexuality. In *Reproducing gender? Essays on educational theory and feminist politics* (pp. 41–53). London: Routledge-Falmer.

Banks, J. (1994). *An introduction to multicultural education*. Needham Heights, MA: Allyn & Bacon.

Bell, L. A. (1997). Theoretical foundations for social justice education. In M. Adams, L. Bell & P. Griffin (Eds.), *Teaching for diversity and social justice* (pp. 3–15). New York: Routledge.

Bem, S. (1993). *The Lenses of gender: Transforming the debate on sexual inequality*. New Haven: Yale University Press.

Blaise, M. (2005). *Playing it straight!: Uncovering gender discourses in the early childhood classroom*. New York: Routledge Press.

Blount, J. M. (1996, Summer). Manly men and womanly women: Deviance, gender role polarization, and the shift in women's school employment, 1900–1976. *Harvard Educational Review*, 66 (2), 318–338.

Blount, J. M. (2005). *Fit to teach: Same-sex desire, gender, and school work in the twentieth century*. Albany, NY: SUNY Press.

Bornstein, K. (1997). Preface. In C. Queen & L. Schimel (Eds.), *Pomosexuals: Challenging assumptions about gender and sexuality* (pp. 13–17). San Francisco: Cleis Press, Inc.

Britzman, D. (1995). Is there a queer pedagogy? or, stop reading straight. *Educational Theory*, 45 (2), 151–165.

Britzman, D. (2000). Precocious education. In S. Talburt & S. Steinberg (Eds.), *Thinking queer: Sexuality, culture, and education* (pp. 33–60). New York: Peter Lang.

Britzman, D., & Gilbert, J. (2004). What will have been said about gayness in teacher education. *Teaching Education*, 15 (1), 81–96.

Butler, J. (1990). *Gender trouble*. New York: Routledge Falmer.

California Safe Schools Coalition. (2004). *Consequences of harassment based on actual or perceived sexual orientation and gender non-conformity and steps for making schools safer*. Davis: University of California.

Chase, C. (2003). Hermaphrodites with attitude: Mapping the emergence of intersex political activism. In R. J. Corber & S. Valocchi (Eds.), *Queer studies: An interdisciplinary reader* (pp. 31–45). Malden, MA: Blackwell.

Craig, W. M., Pepler, D.J., Jiang, D., & Connolly, J. (in preparation). Victimization in children and adolescents: A developmental and relational perspective. Retrieved March 20, 2009, from http://prevnet.ca/Bullying/BullyingStatistics/tabid/122/Default.aspx

Dijkstra, J. K., Lindenberg, S., & Veenstra, R. (2007). Same-gender and cross-gender peer acceptance and peer rejection and their relation to bullying and helping among preadolescents: Comparing predictions from gender-homophily and goal-framing approaches. *Developmental Psychology*, 43 (6), 1377–1389.

Ennis, R. (1976). Equality of educational opportunity. *Educational Theory*, 26, 3–18.

Fausto-Sterling, A. (2000). *Sexing the body: Gender politics and the construction of sexuality*. New York: Basic Books.

Feinberg, L. (1993). *Stone butch blues*. Amherst, New York: Firebrand Books.

Feinberg, L. (1998). Allow me to introduce myself. In *Transliberation: Beyond pink or blue*. Boston: Beacon Press.

Fraser, J. (1996). Democracy. In J. J. Chambliss (Ed.), *Philosophy of education: An encyclopedia* (pp. 139–143). New York and London: Garland Publishing.

Friend, R. (1993). Choices, not closets: Heterosexism and homophobia in schools. In L. Weis & M. Fine (Eds.), *Beyond silenced voices: Class, race, and gender in United States schools* (pp. 209–235). Albany, NY: State University of New York Press.

Friere, P. (1970/1993). *Pedagogy of the oppressed*. New York: Continuum.

Giroux, H. (1991). Modernism, postmodernism and feminism: Rethinking the boundaries of educational discourse. In *Postmodernism, feminism, and cultural politics* (pp. 1–59). Albany, NY: SUNY Press.

Giroux, H. (1998). An activist forum V: Racing justice. In W. Ayers, J. A. Hunt & T. Quinn (Eds.), *Teaching for social justice* (pp. 290–291). New York: Teachers College Press.

Graham, S., & Bellmore, A. D. (2007). Peer victimization and mental health during early adolescence. *Theory Into Practice*, 46 (2), 138–146.

Gramsci, A. (1971/1995). *Further selections from the prison notebooks* (D. Boothman, Trans.). Minneapolis, MN: University of Minnesota Press.

Gramsci, A. (1995). *Further selections from the prison notebooks* (D. Boothman, Trans.). Minneapolis, MN: University of Minnesota Press.

Greene, M. (1998). Introduction: teaching for social justice. In W. Ayers, J. A. Hunt & T. Quinn (Eds.), *Teaching for social justice* (pp. xxvii–xlvi). New York: Teachers College Press.

Gruber, J. E., & Fineran, S. (2007). The Impact of bullying and sexual harassment on middle and high school girls. *Violence Against Women*, 13 (6), 627–643.

Gutman, A. (1987). *Democratic education*. Princeton, NJ: Princeton University Press.

hooks, b. (1994). *Teaching to transgress: Education as the practice of freedom*. New York: Routledge-Falmer.

Howe, K. (1997). *Understanding equal educational opportunity: Social justice and democracy in schooling*. New York: Teacher's College Press.

Jagose, A. (1996). *Queer theory: An introduction*. New York: New York University Press.

Kanpol, B. (1994). *Critical pedagogy: An introduction*. Westport, CT: Bergin & Garvey.

Kellner, D. (2009). *Guys and guns amok*. Boulder, CO: Paradigm Publishers.

Kimmel, M. S., & Mahler, M. (2003). Adolescent masculinity, homophobia, and violence: random school shootings, 1982–2001. *American Behavioral Scientist*, 46 (10), 1439–1458.

Renold, E. (2000). Coming out: Gender (hetero)sexuality and the primary school. *Gender and Education*, 12(3), 309–326.

Renold, E. (2003). If you don't kiss me you're dumped: Boys, boyfriends and heterosexualised masculinities in the primary school. *Educational Review*, 55(2), 179–194.

Renold, E. (2006). "They won't let us play ... Unless you're going out with one of them": Girls, boys and butler's "Heterosexual matrix" in the primary years. *British Journal of Sociology of Education*, 27 (4), 489–509.

Rich, A. (1978/1993). Compulsory heterosexuality and lesbian existence. In H. Abelove, D. Halperin & M. A. Barale (Eds.), *The Lesbian and gay studies reader* (pp. 227–254). New York: Routledge.

Rigby, K., & Slee, P. (1999). Suicidal ideation among adolescent school children, involvement in bully-victim problems, and perceived social support. *Suicide and Life-Threatening Behavior*, 29 (2), 119–130.

Russell, S. T., McGuire, J.K., Laub, C., Manke, E., O'Shaughnessy, M., Heck, K., & et al. (2006). *Harassment in school based on actual or perceived sexual orientation*. San Francisco, CA: California Safe Schools Coalition.

Sedgwick, E. K. (1990/1993). Epistemology of the closet. In H. Abelove, M. A. Barale & D. M. Halperin (Eds.), *The Lesbian and gay studies reader* (pp. 45–61). New York: Routledge.

Setoodeh, R. (2008, July 28). Young, gay and murdered. *Newsweek, CLII*, 40–46.

Slee, P. (1995). Bullying: Health concerns of Australian secondary school students. *International Journal of Adolescence & Youth*, 5 (4), 215–224.

Sleeter, C., & Grant, C. (1994). *Making choices for multicultural education: Five approaches to race, class and gender*. Toronto, ON: Maxwell Macmillan Canada.

Steinberg, S. (Ed.). (2009). *Diversity and multiculturalism: A reader*. New York: Peter Lang.

Stoudt, B. G. (2006). You're either in or you're out: School violence, peer discipline, and the (re)production of hegemonic masculinity. *Men and Masculinities*, 8 (3), 273–287.

Szlacha, L. (2003). Safer sexual diversity climates: Lessons learned from an evaluation of Massachusetts safe schools program for gay and lesbian students. *American Journal of Education*, 110 (1), 58–88.

van Wormer, K., & McKinney, R. (2003). What schools can do to help gay/lesbian/bisexual youth: A harm reduction approach. *Adolescence*, 38 (151), 409.

Weiler, K. (2001). Rereading paulo friere. In K. Weiler (Ed.), *Feminist engagements: Reading, resisting, and revisioning male theorists in education and cultural studies* (pp. 67–87). New York: Routledge.

Weis, L., & Fine, M. (Eds.). (2005). *Beyond silenced voices: Class, race, and gender in United States schools*(Rev. ed.). Albany, NY: State University of New York Press.

West, C., & Zimmerman, D. H. (1987). Doing gender. *Gender and Society*, 1 (2), 125–151.

Westheimer, J., & Kahne, J. (1998). Education for action: Preparing youth for participatory democracy. In W. Ayers, J. A. Hunt & T. Quinn (Eds.), *Teaching for social justice* (pp. 1–20). New York: Teachers College Press.

Wilchins, R. A. (1997). Lines in the sand, cries of desire. In C. Queen & L. Schimel (Eds.), *Pomosexuals: Challenging assumptions about gender and sexuality* (pp. 138–149). San Francisco: Cleis Press.

Young, A. J., & Middleton, M. J. (2002). The gay ghetto in the geography of education textbooks. In R. Kissen (Ed.), *Getting ready for Benjamin: Preparing teachers for sexual diversity in the classroom* (pp. 91–102). Lanham, MD: Rowman Littlefield.

Young, R., & Sweeting, H. (2004). Adolescent bullying, relationships, psychological Well-Being, and gender-atypical behavior: A gender diagnosticity approach. *Sex Roles: A Journal of Research*, 50, 7–8.

Chapter 2
Understanding Sex and Gender

Myths and misconceptions about sex and gender:
(1) Sex and gender are two words that can be used interchangeably.
(2) There are only two sexes and two genders.
(3) The sex assigned at birth always predicts a person's gender identity.
(4) The way children are raised is the strongest influence on their gender identity.

2.1 Introduction

The myths and misconceptions about sex and gender listed above guide the discussion and goals for this chapter. In order to best address these myths and misconceptions, the terms sex and gender are defined and discussed in depth using case studies and real-life examples to help the reader form a more nuanced understanding of these concepts. As this book hopes to point out, it is the presence of a narrow sex/gender binary system that is the source of difficulty for many individuals – not their own identity or embodiment.

The terms "sex" and "gender" are commonly used interchangeably in everyday conversation. Sex and gender describe two different but closely related concepts that describe aspects of our bodies and identities and how they act and interact with the bodies and identities of others in our society. Some professionals including medical doctors, counselors, educators, and researchers misuse the terms; this contributes to popular confusion of the concepts of sex and gender. This chapter aims to clarify these terms and help provide the reader a more nuanced and complex understanding of these concepts in order to improve the experiences of all students in schools.

Most people have been taught to see the world as divided into two halves: male and female. Unfortunately, this division that is taught from the moment a child is conceived is an oversimplification that ends up inflicting a great deal of pain and suffering on many people. Although many human beings are comfortable in and proud of their male and female bodies, and their gender identities, there are many individuals who are not as comfortable in or proud of their bodies or identities due to the narrow definitions of sex and gender our society has created.

E.J. Meyer, *Gender and Sexual Diversity in Schools*, Explorations of Educational Purpose 10, DOI 10.1007/978-90-481-8559-7_2, © Springer Science+Business Media B.V. 2010

Although most of this chapter is dedicated to clarifying the concepts of sex and gender and the variety of approaches to understanding these categories, it is important to note that I feel it is less essential to understand *why* there is such variation than it is to understand *how* to respect and appreciate this diversity. If we focus on too much on *why* then we are asking the wrong questions based in faulty assumptions. It is more important to think about *how* educators and other youth workers can create more effective and inclusive schools, classrooms, and community spaces. However, in order to offer educators and youth workers a firm foundation in how sex and gender is understood and structured, in order to better teach against prevailing myths and misconceptions, we start with an examination of sex categories.

2.2 Let's Talk About Sex

Sex is a medico-legal category that has been created by doctors and politicians in order to categorize and recognize various types of bodies. Scientists have defined sex as the biological characteristics of an organism related to one's reproductive capacities. These characteristics include one's external genitalia, chromosomal makeup, hormones, and reproductive organs. Sex is also a legal category that is regulated by countries as every individual is assigned an official sex and must go through lengthy physical and psychological processes to secure permission to formally change how they are legally recognized. Historically animal organisms have been divided into two categories: male and female, even though there are organisms that don't fit clearly into these categories. Some species have what the scientific community have named hermaphrodites. These are organisms that either have the reproductive capacity of both male and female at the same time, or can transform from one to the other depending on the needs of the population. In human beings, "true" hermaphrodites are incredibly rare although there are many variations of maleness and femaleness that don't fit any of the above terms. I use this term here because it is one that many people may be familiar with. However, it is important to note that this is not the preferred or scientifically accurate term for human beings who are born with physical characteristics that are recognized as both male and female.

When a baby is born, it is assigned a sex at birth usually based on the appearance of its external genitalia. If there is a penis, it is declared to be a boy; if there is a vagina it is declared to be a girl. This is then marked on the child's birth certificate and the parents raise that child according to the social expectations for a child of that sex. This is also referred to as the "gender of rearing" since family members begin to interact with and socialize the child based on the sex category assigned at birth. Although this process might appear simple and straightforward to the average parent, it does not take into consideration the possible amounts of variation that exist in bodies that have penises and testicles, bodies that have vaginas and ovaries, and bodies that have elements of both. This section will introduce and explore four different sex categories that can be used to understand and describe bodies: *Male, female, intersex,* and *transsexual.*

First let's consider the story of Maria Patino, a track athlete headed to the 1988 Olympics to compete for Spain. She had forgotten her required certificate of femininity and needed to have it verified onsite by the "femininity control head office." This exam determined that she had a Y chromosome and testes in her labia as well as no uterus or ovaries and therefore could not compete as a woman. Another individual named Levi Suydam living in Salisbury, Connecticut, in 1843 petitioned for the right to vote in an important local election. The doctor examined Levi and declared him to be male and eligible to vote. However, a few days later the physician discovered that Levi menstruated regularly and had a vaginal opening (Fausto-Sterling, 2000, pp. 1, 31). These individuals offer a few examples of how sex can be embodied in ways that transcend the narrowly defined categories of male and female. These are both examples of individuals who would now be recognized as intersex.

A fourth sexual category is known as transsexualism. This occurs when an individual's physical characteristics, or *phenotype*, are recognized as male or female, but that person's identity doesn't align with their biological sex so they undergo medical treatments such as hormone therapy and/or surgery to transform their body to match one's social identity (GIRES, 2006). Some may believe that this is a relatively recent concept or experience, however, this term first emerged in 1949 in the work, *psychopathia transsexualis,* by David O. Cauldwell (Sullivan, 2003, p. 102). One of the earliest public figures to speak about her sex reassignment surgery was Christine Jorgensen in 1952; scholars suggest that there is evidence of such surgical interventions as early as 1882 (Sullivan, 2003). How sex is decided at that moment of birth is not as straightforward and reliable as our high school biology textbooks led us to believe. The next section presents a brief scientific overview of how bodies develop and are categorized.

2.2.1 Sex Determination 101

There are three main factors that shape how the human body develops sexually: chromosomes, gonads, and hormones. *Chromosomal sex* is determined by ovum and sperm that combine their genetic material to create a new organism. The egg (ovum) always contributes an X chromosome, and the sperm contributes either an X or a Y. Females develop from XX sex chromosomes and males develop from XY chromosomes. These are the first factors that impact the process of *sex determination* (Smith, 2007, p. 200). In rare cases, children are born with different chromosomal combinations including XO (*Turner Syndrome*) and XXY (*Klinefelter Syndrome*), which impact their sexual development. These are discussed in greater detail in the section on intersex people.

Gonadal Sex describes the type of sexual organs that develop in an organism: ovaries, testes, or a combination of both. Most *ovaries* produce estrogen, progestin, and ova and most *testes* produce steroid hormones and sperm. Early in development, the gonadal tissue is undifferentiated. If a Y chromosome is present, it stimulates production of *Testis Determination Factor (TDF)* protein which causes testes to develop. In the absence of this protein, ovaries develop. In other words, all embryos start as female and will develop as such unless TDF is present to create testes.

The third influence in the sexual development of a child is hormones. *Hormonal sex* is determined by the levels of chemical produced by the endocrine glands. These shape the development of internal organs and external genitalia. All bodies produce estrogen, progesterone, and testosterone, but at different levels and they impact bodies in different ways. If a Y chromosome is present and testes have formed, they begin to secrete hormones that prevent a uterus and vagina from developing and stimulate the production of testosterone and the growth of male structures such as a penis and scrotum.

In the majority of births, these three determining factors work together to create a body with a reproductive system that is clearly recognizable as male or female. However, in approximately 1.7% of all births children have a variation on the themes of maleness and femaleness and are intersex (Fausto-Sterling, 2000). This quick review of mammalian biology was intended to help clarify how science has defined the sexes and why it is necessary to expand the categories that exist beyond male and female. This section is not meant to be an exhaustive overview of the science and medicine that have created these categories, as this has been done effectively by other authors (Fausto-Sterling, Kessler, GIRES). Instead, I hope to provide a basic framework to help the average parent or educator better understand the multiple factors that are involved in determining and assigning the sex of a body at birth.

2.2.2 How Many Sexes are There?

In a famous and controversial article published in 1993, biologist and feminist Anne Fausto-Sterling made an argument for expanding our sex categories from two to five (Fausto-Sterling, 1993). Her five categories included males, females, herms ("true" hermaphrodites), merms (male "pseudo-hermaphrodites"), and ferms (female "pseudo-hermaphrodites"). This article produced a firestorm of debate, and although Fausto-Sterling no longer advocates for such a system (Fausto-Sterling, 2000, p. 110), she argues for expanding our notions of maleness and femaleness and not limiting our definitions of these terms to the size and shape of a person's genitals. She supports a position advanced by Suzanne Kessler who believes that giving "genitals primary signifying status ignores the fact that in the everyday world gender attributions are made without access to genital inspection...what has primacy in everyday life is the gender that is performed, regardless of the flesh's configuration under the clothes" (Kessler, 1998, p. 90). I support this argument as it emphasizes the importance of understanding how gender – the way we identify and are socially recognized – has greater day-to-day importance than our sex, however, there are important descriptive terms that can help us understand the variability in the sexes. I propose the following four terms to help us understand the different bodies and sexual categories that are currently used. These categories were selected due to their use in research and activist communities, and the fact that we currently rely heavily on such medico-legal categories to organize and understand bodies and how they interact in the world: *male, female, transsexual*, and *intersex*. Although these terms are contested and imperfect, in the interests of developing a shared introductory vocabulary, they are what I propose for now.

As explained earlier, there are three main biological systems that contribute to creating the sex of an individual. For females, they have an XX *genotype*, their *genitals* (external sex organs) include a vagina, clitoris, and labia; their *gonads* (internal sex organs) include ovaries and a uterus; and their bodies produce the hormones oestrogen and progesterone in quantities that cause their bodies to ovulate, menstruate, potentially support a pregnancy, and nurse a newborn. Since reproduction of the species is the primary reason for biological sex differentiation, the key elements of the sexed body are related to procreating. Does this mean that women who are XX and have vaginas, but aren't able to get pregnant are less female? That XY men with penises who don't produce sperm, or can't ejaculate are less male? I pose these questions here in order to encourage the reader to being to critique the way biology and scientific discourse have shaped and limited our thinking.

The biological definition of *male* refers to an individual who has an XY genotype, genitalia that includes a penis and scrotum, gonads that include testes, and a body that produces androgens (primarily testosterone) in sufficient amounts through the lifespan to produce and emit sperm. As mentioned earlier, the default developmental path is for an embryo to become female. Very specific structures need to be in place for a ball of cells to differentiate and grow to become a reproductively mature male. Researchers believe that this is one of the main reasons that female embryos and fetuses are healthier than male embryos and fetuses. There are higher rates for *teratogenic* birth defects and behavioral problems (related to harmful substances such as alcohol, drugs, and chemicals), spontaneous abortions, and still-births in male babies than for female babies. The Y chromosome carries fewer genes and therefore has a weaker defense system (Smith, 2007, p. 204).

The third sex category, *transsexuals*, includes individuals who have either an XX or XY genotype as well as the associated phenotypic traits for their genetic sex but have a gender identity that does not align with their physical sexual characteristics. This contradiction of physical and psychological traits has been termed *gender dysphoria* by the medical profession. Transsexuals are usually assigned the clinical label Gender Identity Disorder (GID) in the Diagnostic and Statistical Manual of Mental Disorders (DSM-IV) of the American Psychiatric Association, although activists have been trying to get this condition removed from the DSM. As the lead character in the film *TransAmerica* so eloquently argued, "If it can be fixed with plastic surgery, is it really a mental disorder" (Tucker, 2005)? Some transsexual men and women choose to undergo a series of medical treatments to realign their physical characteristics with their internal identity. These treatments generally include hormone injections and surgery (GIRES et al., 2006, p. 29).

There is as much diversity among transsexual people as there are among male, female, and intersex people. There is no single path to living as a transsexual person. Some transsexuals talk about their process in terms of the interventions that they have chosen to undertake including *non-operative, pre-operative, transitioning,* and *post-operative* individuals. These descriptions identify where in the physical transformation process their bodies are situated. Transsexuals, by definition, are individuals who have chosen to undergo some physical changes in order to be recognized as belonging to a sex category other than the one they were assigned at birth. Access to hormones and surgery can be costly and difficult which means that many transsexuals live in bodies that they are not comfortable in or proud of. The social bias and systemic discrimination against these individuals can create many obstacles for them at school, home, and work. Although they may *pass* publicly as the sex that they identify with, they are often *outed* when required for identification purposes to produce a birth certificate or driver's license to register for school or apply for a job. The process for changing these official papers is lengthy and complicated and varies regionally. This is a difficult hurdle that many transsexuals have to face during the challenging and lengthy period of transition and demonstrates the importance of recognizing sex as a legal category as well as a medical or biological one.

Transsexuals may also identify as *MTF* or *FTM*. MTF (male-to-female) transsexuals are individuals who were named as males at birth but are transitioning to live as female. They also may be known as trans-women, or if they have completed all aspects of their transition they may choose only to identify as a woman. FTM (female-to-male) transsexuals are individuals who were categorized as females at birth and are transitioning to live as males. They may also be known as trans-men, or as men. Some transsexual advocates prefer the terminology *FTF* (female-to-female) and *MTM* (male-to-male) which describes the change process from internal identification to external realignment. This is important to many who believe that they have always been the sex that they identify with and want to be fully recognized as such.

The fourth category, *intersex*, describes people whose genotype or phenotype varies from the above definitions of male and female. This is a relatively new category due to the recent emergence of activism around this issue, however, many individuals who have intersex characteristics may not be aware of this or may not identify as such. The term intersex may be used to describe a range of causes for sexual development that is nondimorphic (not clearly male or female). According to one review of the literature, approximately 1.7% of babies born are intersex (Fausto-Sterling, 2000, p. 53). Most of these children were never told about their early medical histories, and this entire category of people had been almost completely erased from society since early surgical interventions allowed doctors to "correct" infants who were born with genitals that were not clearly male or female. Intersex activists and their allies are now working to educate doctors and parents about the risks of early surgery and believe this is a form of genital mutilation (Chase, 2003). Many parents and doctors rush these infants to surgery in order to quickly assign them a male or female sex. Usually these infants are made female because it is more complicated to construct a penis than it is to construct a vagina. Adult intersex activists argue that this early surgery and the lack of information provided to them as teenagers and adults has caused them significant harm and they aim to reduce the numbers of unnecessary surgeries for infants (Preves, 2009). Although intersex people may not be considered *normal*, they are very clearly natural. They are born as they are; they are a product of the variations of nature. Our need to impose izing categories over naturally occurring ones is an example of how the se. imposes artificial, socially created limits on people's lives.

Some common causes of intersex bodies include: *Congenital A_ Hyperplasia*, Klinefelter Syndrome, Turner Syndrome, *Androgen Insens_ _rity Syndrome*, and *Gonadal Dysgenesis* (Fausto-Sterling, 2000, p. 52). In the earlier story about Maria Patino, she was determined to have Androgen Insensitivity Syndrome. She was genetically male (XY), but her body never responded to the hormones her body produced to develop male sex characteristics, therefore she developed as a female who retained her early embryonic male structures.

This brief overview of sex categories and how they are currently understood was presented here to challenge and deepen existing understandings about sex. As mentioned above, our sex categories have very little to do with how we interact with others on a daily basis. In other words, it is hardly necessary for our friends, co-workers, and acquaintances to know our exact gonadal and chromosomal makeup. However, the way these are labeled and linked to cultural notions of gender are incredibly important in shaping how individuals understand and present themselves and interact with others in the social world.

2.3 Let's Talk About Gender (Psychosocial)

When I was in 4th grade, my elementary school gave us the chance to choose a musical instrument to learn to play. I wanted desperately to play the trumpet. It was shiny and loud and could be clearly heard in any musical piece. When I announced to my older brother that I wanted to choose the trumpet he said to me, "You can't play the trumpet, only boys play the trumpet." When the time came to make our selection, I chose an appropriate instrument for a girl: the flute. I always regretted that decision, and wonder how many other opportunities I missed because it was not appropriate for a girl. As noted above, our bodies are sexed based on biological and legal categories, and as this section explains, they are gendered as a result of relationships with ourselves and others in the social world.

Gender is the range of social and relational characteristics that mark our bodies as belonging to one of several social categories. The most common categories are boy/man and girl/woman, but they are not the only possible ones. There are also individuals who identify as transgender, two-spirit, and genderqueer. These terms are defined and examined in this section. Gender is different from, but related to sex. Gender is a complex set of situated relationships that describe how we identify ourselves and how others choose to interact with us in the world. It is informed by the sex that we are assigned at birth, and although many females develop a gender identity as a girl or woman, and many males identify as boys and men, many individuals also develop gender identities that vary from this familiar pattern.

The modern concept of gender emerged in print in 1955 in an article in the *Bulletin Johns Hopkins Hospital* by sex researcher John Money and was later popularized in his book *Man and woman, boy and girl* (1972) (Fausto-Sterling, 2000; Money, 1973). He introduced this term to describe the social patterns that shaped and informed people's experiences in the world. Much initial research and discussion of the concept of gender was done by Money and his colleagues who were working to understand the experiences of transgender and intersex people in Western societies. As this work evolved, it became clear that everyone's experiences in the world were gendered, and one's *gender expression* had a significant impact on one's daily life and long-term opportunities. Gender expression is a term used to describe how one presents oneself to the world through external symbols and behaviors such as clothing, accessories, hairstyle, body language, and tone of voice. This expression is a reflection of our *gender identity*, or how we view ourselves and which gender category we embrace.

The most common gender identities in world cultures are boy/man and girl/woman. In western societies, which in modern times have all been patriarchal, women's and men's roles and identities were historically constructed in opposition to each other. Woman equals not man and man equals not woman. The next section begins by examining masculinity and men's roles before discussing femininity and women's roles to situate historically how these evolved. This is then followed by more recently named gender identities such as transgender, two-spirit, and genderqueer. This is not meant to imply that other gender identities did not exist until recently, only that they have only recently begun to be named and written about by people with access to publishing their ideas in institutionally recognized texts. This section concludes by examining the concept of a gender binary and whether it continues to be relevant or useful in the new millennium.

2.3.1 Boys and Men: Exploring Masculinities

Modern notions of masculinity are informed by historical, social, and cultural influences. Western masculinity theorist Raewyn Connell[1] (1995) suggested four categories of masculinity: hegemonic, complicit, subordinate, and marginalized. She argues masculinity is constructed in relation to and against femininity and subordinated forms of masculinity: "The dominant masculine form is characterized by heterosexuality, power, authority, aggression and technical competence" (Mac an Ghaill, 1995, p. 12). *Hegemonic masculinity* is at the top of a hierarchy of masculinities and is defined by strength, competitiveness, and aggressiveness. As gender theorist Martin Mills points out

> In each of the signifiers of masculinity there is an association of maleness with coercive power. Dominant images of the 'ideal man' portray him as competitive, strong, aggressive when crossed, and as a good 'mate' (mate here referring to friendships between males

---

[1]This work was originally published under the name Robert Connell, however she now goes by Raewyn and uses feminine pronouns.

as opposed to sexual partner). This image is true of the action hero, the football star, the business magnate and even the popular politician. The physical, sexual and, sometimes, intellectual prowess of these heroic men is beyond the reach of most men. However, the ideal forms the basis of hegemonic masculinities. (Mills, 2001, p. 23)

At the other end of the hierarchy of masculinities are those identities deemed as *subordinate*. Men use power over other men to enforce this system and often act with violence toward individuals who are viewed as "traitors to masculinity." The most notable grouping within the category of "subordinate masculinities" are gay men (Mills, 2001, p. 70). Although sexual orientation is different from gender and is explored in greater depth in the next chapter, it clearly impacts how gender is interpreted and understood. Heterosexuality is one of the key elements in hegemonic masculinity.

In between these two extremes of masculinity rest the middle two categories: *complicit* and *marginalized*. Men who inhabit the space of complicit masculinity don't challenge the dominance of hegemonic masculine values in society, and continue to benefit from it. Many boys and men experience this form of masculinity for they do not act out the "worst excesses of hegemonic masculinity," but they do very little to challenge the existing patriarchal gender order and thereby reinforce it. They don't see the harm in how men exercise their male power and often accept it as natural or view harassing behaviors as playful teasing or harmless banter. These men and boys are in unique locations to help undo this hierarchy, but they rarely choose to intervene and interrupt such behaviors for it would then call their own masculinity into question. Finally, *marginalized* masculinities address the many layers of social identity and how male privilege can be mediated by other factors such as race, ethnicity, and dis/ability. For example, Mills looked specifically at the experience of Aboriginal men in Australia and how their cultural background kept them from accessing their male privilege to the extent available to White men. He explains that, "numerous examples abound of non-Anglo and non-middle-class men who become exemplars of hegemonic masculinity within the sporting and entertainment arenas. However, marginality will always impact on the extent of these benefits" (2001, p. 76).

There are opponents to social constructionist theories who try to claim that gender and sex are inextricably linked, and by being born with a "Y" chromosome a child is biologically predisposed to acting in certain ways. Parents and teachers who quickly dismiss boys' overly rambunctious behavior by shaking their heads and saying "boys will be boys" are using this argument. By stating that biology has a stronger hold on behavior than environment, adults are allowing boys to avoid accepting responsibility for their own actions and are reducing the power that they themselves have to influence that child's development in positive ways. This belief is closely tied to the myth that high levels of testosterone results in high levels of violence. Willam Pollack addresses this misunderstanding in his chapter *Real boys: The truths behind the myths*, "[this] idea…stems from the mistaken assumption that testosterone is the only force that inclines boys toward both active, rough-and-tumble play and violent behaviour. This is not the case. Boys do play differently than girls, but their style of play is not solely a function of testosterone and it certainly does not prove a proclivity for violence" (2002, p. 91). He cites several studies that observed how testosterone and other artificial hormones impacted men's behavior, and it is clear that "no simple scientific link has been made between testosterone levels and the tendency for aggression and violence" (92). Just as many hormones and chemicals in our bodies can influence our actions and decision making, testosterone is just one factor among many, and Pollack concludes that, "the level of testosterone in any boy – and the way that testosterone affects him – has less impact on his behavior than how the boy is loved, nurtured, and shaped by his parents and by the context of the society in which he lives" (92). We now turn our attention to girls and women and how femininity has been constructed in relation to the masculinities described above.

2.3.2 Girls and Women – The Second Sex

Simone de Beauvoir's seminal work *The Second Sex* (1949), played a key role in framing modern discussions about women's place in society. In the past 200 years, women in North America have evolved from being considered their fathers' or husbands' property (Rubin, 1975) to being recognized as full and equal independent citizens who are now able own property, vote, get an education, and choose to not marry or to select their own spouses. Traditional notions of femininity have always been closely affiliated with a stratified class society. The ability to avoid manual labor, attend to fashion and one's physical appearance, and learn to be "ladylike" was primarily available to women in the upper classes. Although there are many variations of femininity that have emerged in modern times due to the work of feminist activists, there are still some common threads that unite notions of femininity. One culturally valued aspect of femininity includes being desirable to men: choosing hairstyles, makeup, and clothing that highlight their heterosexual appeal. This is another example of how gender and sexual orientation are at once interrelated and distinct identity categories. Another culturally valued aspect of femininity includes nurturing and taking care of others, which has been linked to the biological role of the mother/creator of life (Bem, 1993; De Beauvoir, 1949). These expectations are repeatedly taught and reinforced through books, television and other mass media, family life, peer relationships, and school.

Although forms of valued femininity vary across, racial, ethnic, and class lines (Brown, 2005; O'Connor, Lewis, & Mueller, 2005), all forms of femininity are devalued in comparison to masculinity in patriarchal cultures (Meyer, 2006). The practice of misogyny, or devaluing of the feminine, effectively limits the opportunities of those with a highly feminine gender identity or expression. Although many women have been able to secure social and economic success by navigating this heteronormative hierarchy, there still exist limits on the diversity of role models and opportunities available to girls and young women. These limits also close off the opportunity for a diverse understanding of gender that goes beyond either masculine for boys or feminine for girls. There is a great diversity of masculinities and femininities that include people who identify as men and women but are recognized as androgynous or gender non-conforming. In addition to these gender variations, there are other identities such as transgender, two-spirit, and genderqueer. The next sections explore these gender identities and expressions that are often invisible or ignored.

2.3.3 Transgender: Transcending Gender

The word *transgender* entered the English language in the 1980s from the transsexual and transvestite communities (Cromwell, 1997, p. 134) to describe individuals who are not *cisgender*, or whose gender identity is different from the sex that they were assigned at birth. Cisgender is a term used to describe individuals whose gender identity and expression align with cultural notions associated with their sex assigned at birth. There are many myths and misconceptions about transgender individuals, and there is as much variety of gender expression within the transgender community as there is within groups of men and women. Some transgender people strongly embrace traditional notions of gender and proudly live as highly feminine or highly masculine people. Other transgender people choose to challenge and disrupt the categories of masculinity and femininity and embrace varying degrees of each (Bornstein, 1998; Califia, 1997; Feinberg, 1998; Wilchins, 1997). According to some research, only 23% of children who experience tension between their assigned sex at birth (and thus, their gender of rearing), and their own gender identity are transsexuals who choose to undergo physical transformations (Smith, Van Goozen, & Cohen-Kettenis, 2001). Some won't have surgery and hormone treatments because of the expense and challenge in securing approval, and others may not because they are uncomfortable with the risks and limitations of surgery and many are happy with their bodies as they are.

The medical profession labels transgender people as having "atypical gender development" or "gender dysphoria" according to the Diagnostic and Statistical Manual of Mental Disorders of the American Psychiatric Association (GIRES, 2006). There are mixed feelings about these categories and their impacts on the health and safety of transgender people. On one hand, these diagnostic classifications can provide access to funds to pay for therapy and surgery to individuals who are transsexual and who meet the criteria. On the other hand, these categories pathologize these individuals as "mentally ill" and thus subject them to discrimination. It is also possible that some transgender individuals are also intersex and have had a developmental pathway that is different from the average male or female child (GIRES, 2006). Although the similarities and the differences between transgender, transsexual, and intersex are complex and nuanced, it is important to take a moment to be sure you understand these differences so as not to perpetuate stereotypes and misinformation. The key factor is to focus on the central differences identified in this chapter between sex and gender in order to understand the distinction between transgender and transsexual people.

One is a gender identity; the second is a medically recognized category. There is much overlap between the two categories: all transsexuals are transgender, however, not all transgender people are transsexual. In spite of the risk of oversimplifying

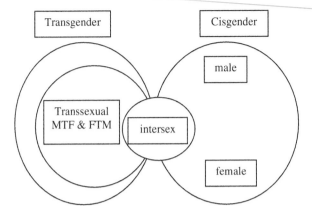

Fig 2.1 Sex and gender

these concepts, I created a diagram to help the reader conceptualize these separate, but interrelated notions of sex and gender (Fig 2.1).

2.3.4 Two-Spirit: Aboriginal Identities

A fourth gender category that has emerged in North America is *two-spirit*. This term is used to describe people who are alternatively gendered and are members of Native American (also known as Amerindian, First Nations, Inuit, and Métis) communities. It replaces the earlier term, berdache, used by anthropologists who studied these cultures (Lang, 1997, p. 100). Early anthropologists often misunderstood the spiritual element of the two-spirit individual and described it as a form of institutionalized male homosexuality. As more recent authors have pointed out, becoming a berdache was more related to occupational preferences and social roles than sexual behavior (Lang, 1997, p. 101). The term two-spirit is an attempt at creating an English-language term that best describes a cultural concept of gender that differs from the western binary. This chapter cannot adequately describe all the variations of two-spirit people from the different North American Native communities (Blackwood, 1997, p. 289), therefore it is important to acknowledge that the information presented here is partial and intended to provide the reader with a brief introduction to the concept. For more detailed information, please refer to the authors cited in this section.

The term two-spirit was chosen since many of the terms in Native American languages for these individuals describe some sort of combination of the masculine and feminine (Shoshoni). Other languages use terms that describe a process of constant change (Navajo, Sioux) (Lang, 1997, p. 103). Some theorists think this term is inadequate and imbued with the western dichotomy by the use of the number "two" (Kehoe, 1997, p. 269). Due to the effects of colonization and Christianization, most of these cultures were forced to adapt to White western ways of knowing and the presence of and respect for two-spirit people was lost. Modern BGLQT people from First Nations communities have turned to the concept of the two-spirit individual as a historical role model, therefore its modern use can include people of diverse sexual orientations as well as gender identities (Lang, 1997, p. 109). One two-spirit researcher explains, "Two-spirit is not a 'traditional' term, and if it were it could be traditional only for one or a few nations. It is an example of the vitality of contemporary First Nations cultures, expressing for these persons a mode shared across the diversity of their native nations" (Kehoe, 1997, p. 270). Also, at the core of this term is a strong adherence to traditional ways of being and connections to one's identity as an aboriginal or First Nations person. As scholar Sabine Lang points out, "two-spirit people tend to emphasize their Indian/Native American identity and the special potential and skills they as lesbians and gays can contribute for the benefit of the community at large" (1997, p. 115).

2.3.5 Genderqueer: Youth and Postmodern Identities

This newer term is one that has emerged in transgender and gender advocacy organizations to further challenge the existing binaries of how we conceptualize and embody gender. As of this writing, this term is not currently listed in any major dictionaries such as The Oxford English Dictionary, The American Heritage Dictionary, and The Canadian Oxford Dictionary, but has been documented online and in print since 2001 (Hart, 2003; Nestle, Howell, & Wilchins, 2002). Genderqueer is an identity that has been embraced by individuals who feel that their gender identity does not fit clearly in the man/woman binary, even if they have undergone some physical transformations to make their body fit more closely within a male or female form.

Some terms that people have created to describe themselves in this category include genderqueer, trans*(-sexual, -gender, -genderist, -vestite, -cended, -sensual, etc.), gender-gifted, genderqueerriffic, gender-fabulous, gender-plus, gender-more, androgyne, bi-gender(ed), boigirl, girlboi, boygirl, boydyke, girlboy, girlfag, guydyke, pansexual, polysexual, omnisexual, bisexual, transguy, transboi, transdyke, transwoman, FTM, FTMTF, MTF, polygender, intergender, third-gendered, multi-gendered, intersex, straight-but-not-narrow, omnigender, gendertuck, gender-variant, no-ho, no-op (no hormone, no surgery), genderless, metagender(ed), both man and woman, neither man nor woman, effeminate, feminine, femme, butch, masculine, male, queer, gay, lesbian, bi, birl, byke, dyke, open, crossdresser, en femme, in "boy mode," in "girl mode," drag king, drag queen, gender performance artist, gender impressionist, gender bender, gender blender (Alter, Dennis, & Yoo, 2005; Beemyn, 2005). This varied list of identities and experiences in combination with the rich connections and information that can be accessed on the Internet has provided a fertile ground for many people to challenge and further explore their own gender identities. Social networking sites, blogs, and other online support and information sites have given strength and voice to this newly emerging gender identity which explicitly defies any categorization.

2.3.6 Gender Identity Disorder: Challenging the Binary

Gender Identity Disorder, which is related to *gender dysphoria* (depression and anxiety related to one's gender) and *atypical gender identity*, is a medical diagnosis used by doctors and psychologists to label transgender people and their experiences. It is described in the DSM-IV as including four key elements: (1) a strong persistent cross-gender identification; (2) persistent discomfort with his or her sex or sense of inappropriateness in the gender role of that sex; (3) the disturbance is not concurrent with physical intersex condition; and (4) the disturbance causes clinically significant distress or impairment in social, occupational, or other important areas of functioning ("DSM-IV-TR Diagnostic Criteria For Gender Identity Disorder," 2003).

The use of the term "disorder" has been greatly contested by psychiatrists (Hausman, 2003) as well as trans and queer activists such as Kate Bornstein who wrote that "transsexuality is the only condition for which the therapy is to lie" (1994). A transgender advocacy website argues, "It is time for the medical professions to affirm that difference is not disease, nonconformity is not pathology, and uniqueness is not illness" (http://www.transgender.org/gidr/index.html). This phenomenon has been studied by physicians and scientists for over a century. The term atypical gender development is a more recent label used by researchers to describe individuals who develop a gender identity that is not aligned with the sex they were assigned at birth. As stated in the introduction, it is the presence of the narrow sex/gender binary system that is the source of difficulty for many individuals – not their own identity or embodiment. North American and many world cultures are dependent on the heterosexual nuclear family structure for economic reasons (Rubin, 1975) and for social control (Rubin, 1984/1993). Maintaining the two-sex system is in the interest of many political, economic, and religious institutions, but enacts psychological and physical harm on many individuals. It is for this reason that I urge parents, educators, and youth workers to learn to think beyond these boundaries when working with youth in order to better meet their needs. In order to better understand how our current conceptions of gender have evolved, it is important to learn about prevailing theories of gender development. The next section provides a brief summary of these theories.

2.4 Gender Identity Development Theories

Scholars and researchers have been working to develop explanations for variations in gender identity even before a distinct term for it existed. The concept of gender was often referred to as "sex role" as it attempted to differentiate biological differences from social ones. This section provides an introduction to some of the main theories that attempt to explain how children develop their gender identities.

2.4.1 Biological Explanations

One approach to explaining the variety of gender identities that exist in children is to base it solely in the biology of the human organism: hormones, chromosomes, and gonads. One of the earliest proponents of this approach was E. O. Wilson who advanced his theory of sociobiology in his 1975 work, *Sociobiology: The new synthesis*. He argued strongly for his belief that gender-related behaviors were linked to genetic differences alone (Smith, 2007, p. 132). This perspective has been advanced by more recent popular scientists such as Leonard Sax in his book, *Why gender matters: What parents and teachers need to know about the emerging science of sex differences* (2005). As the title indicates, Sax makes no distinction in his book between sex and gender and actively tries to discredit any point of view that allows for environmental or social factors to explain any variation in gender identity and expression. Although Sax makes some compelling arguments about the biological bases for some variation in gender identity and expression, the refusal to acknowledge environmental factors is a major shortcoming of a pure biological approach.

2.4.2 Psychodynamic Explanations

Psychodynamic explanations are those that are based in biological understandings of the brain and body but do recognize that the environment exerts some influence in a child's development. In the psychodynamic schools of thought, there are two prevailing explanations for gender variations: (1) Freudian psychoanalytical and (2) Cognitive Developmental. In Freud's explanations for gender variance, he believed that gender identity emerged out of a child's mirroring of the behaviors of the same-sex parent through a biologically motivated process (Smith, 2007). Among Freud's more well-known theories include the Male Oedipal complex and the Female Electra complex. These theories attempt to explain children's behavior in psychosexual terms where boys see their fathers as sexual rivals for their mothers' attention. Related to this is the fear of castration when they notice that other bodies do not have penises. Freud used this understanding of boys' bodies to attempt to explain girls' behaviors as grounded first in penis envy then in identification with the mother and seeking her father's attention.

Freud's emphasis on the role of the mother and father as the primary influences on children's gender and sexual development is the source of many misconceptions about sex, gender, and sexuality. Although his theories advanced public discourse and additional research into these issues, they were not without controversy. He did recognize the role of social factors in the development of a child, but his primary focus was on male children and many feminist critiques point out the shortcomings of Freudian theory to adequately explain girls' lives and experiences. The field of psychoanalysis has continued to evolve and there are many new and shifting applications of Freud's theories; however, there is insufficient room in this volume to go beyond this brief introduction.

The second psychodynamic approach to understanding gender is based in the work of Lawrence Kohlberg. Kohlberg's work was heavily influenced by Piaget's stage theory of child development. He believed that a child's gender identity was key for sex-role development (Kohlberg, 1966). He asserted that the child's gender identity evolved in the preoperational stage by being able to first label others as "girls" or "boys," second by being able to understand gender stability, or the concept that gender does not change if a person changes their clothes, hair, or location. This generally happens near the end of preoperations and before the concrete operations period. The final step in Kohlberg's theory occurs during the concrete operational period and is that of gender constancy. Kohlberg argues that this is when an individual has developed a coherent and permanent understanding of their own gender (Berndt, 1992; Kohlberg, 1966). Kohlberg's approach asserts that children socialize themselves into exhibiting behaviors consistent with their gender once they have mastered the concepts of gender roles that they have been taught. Although Piaget's developmental theory has proven to be helpful in understanding certain types of children's behaviors, in this arena there are some shortcomings. For example, if one applied Kohlberg's theory to gender non-conforming and transgender children, the conclusion would be that these individuals have cognitive delays that prevent them from synthesizing and applying information that has been presented to them about gender. This explanation has not been supported by research evidence and has been firmly rejected by trans activists and other leaders in this field (Bornstein, 1994, 1998; Feinberg, 1998).

2.4.3 Sociological Explanations

The third area of work that seeks to explain gender identity development is social learning theory, which is based primarily in sociological or cultural explanations. Sandra Bem, a leading scholar in the field of social learning theory, developed a gender schema theory in response to Kohlberg's cognitive-developmental approach. Bem explains her theory as follows:

> Gender schema theory contains two fundamental presuppositions about the process of individual gender formation: first, that there are gender lenses embedded in cultural discourse and social practice that are internalized by the developing child, and second, that once these gender lenses have been internalized, they predispose the child, and later the adult, to construct an identity that is consistent with them. . .This model of enculturation is sufficiently general to explain how all cultural lenses are transferred to the individual, not just gender lenses. (Bem, 1993, p. 139)

Although Bem recognizes the role of the child's cognitive abilities to process information, she emphasizes that gender is learned through social processes and that this sorting is a social phenomenon that is not natural or innate. She also recognizes that the categories of masculine and feminine are culturally specific and the ways that gender is learned and expressed are based in that individual's social experiences not in any biological or essential cognitive process. Bem's theory asserts that if a society can de-gender objects, clothing, behaviors, and other signifiers, then that society could more likely achieve gender equality.

2.4.4 Developmental Systems Theory

The final theory for sex and gender difference presented here is one that seeks to integrate the knowledge and strengths of each of these approaches to explaining sex, gender, and their variations. Developmental Systems Theory (DST) is an integrated approach to understanding sex and gender that pays attention to the influences of biology and sociology, nature and nurture. Anne Fausto-Sterling advocates for this approach in her book, *Sexing the body: Gender politics and the construction of sexuality* (2000). Fausto-Sterling explains that developmental systems theorists reject the dividing of influences into either biological or sociological, and recognizes that these forces work together to shape each individual in distinct ways. Bodies will develop and grow very differently, and that is due to environmental factors such as diet, climate, education, family setting, and health care. DST approaches ask us to stop thinking in terms of "false dichotomies" whether it is those of male/female or nature/nurture. We must seek to understand the connections that happen when these forces interact and appreciate the vast diversity of bodies and identities that are created and shaped by multiple factors.

This theory aligns best with educational approaches grounded in critical pedagogy, feminist, anti-oppressive, and queer theories. In order to encourage critical thinking and to work toward social justice, educators and other youth workers need to model alternative gender formations and encourage creative questioning of oppressive systems. By challenging the hegemony of the rigid sex/gender categories that society has created to organize and control bodies, we can develop more creative and human ways to support and understand the diversity of bodies and experiences that are present in schools and society.

2.5 Conclusion

Each individual has an inherent predisposition (orientation) that influences their expression and performance of gender (behavior) and helps shape how they name themselves and understand who they are in the social world (identity). These three categories (orientation, behavior, and identity) will also be discussed in the context of sexuality in the next chapter. For the majority of people, the sex one is assigned at birth informs one's behavior and identity and if this is the case one is considered cisgender, and therefore, "normal." As a result, cisgender people are never forced to question one's sex or one's gender. As this chapter has indicated, this is not the case for all people and it seems clear that our current medical, linguistic, and political system that is built around the sex/gender binary is inadequate to describe and fully include the true diversity that exists in human nature and therefore must be reconsidered.

Although most of this chapter was dedicated to clarifying the concepts of sex and gender and the variety of approaches to understanding these categories, it is important to reiterate a point made in the introduction of this chapter. I feel it is less important to understand *why* there is such variation in sex and gender than it is to understand *how* to respect and appreciate this diversity. If we focus on *why* then we are asking the wrong questions based in faulty assumptions. This is how the hegemony of science reproduces what we already want to know: by asking questions in ways that reinforce our current understandings of the world. This book aims to help readers work through the *how*. Chapters 4–7 seek to offer readers strategies and approaches to improving how schools can teach this respect and appreciation for all kinds of gender and sexual diversity.

References

Alter, R. L., Dennis, M. M., & Yoo, A. (2005). Genderqueer revolution.Retrieved October 17, 2007, from http://www.genderqueerrevolution.org/

Beemyn, B. (2005). Genderqueer. In C. J. Summers (Ed.), *Glbtq: An encyclopedia of gay, lesbian, bisexual, transgender, and queer culture* (online ed.). Chicago, IL.

Bem, S. (1993). *The lenses of gender: Transforming the debate on sexual inequality*. New Haven: Yale University Press.

Berndt, T. J. (1992). *Child development*. Forth Worth, TX: Harcourt Brace Jovanovich.

Blackwood, E. (1997). Native american genders and sexualities: Beyond anthropological models and misrepresentations. In S.-E. Jacobs, W. Thomas & S. Lang (Eds.), *Two spirit people: Native American gender identity, sexuality, and spirituality* (pp. 284–294). Chicago, IL: University of Illinois Press.

Bornstein, K. (1994). *Gender outlaw: On men, women and the rest of us*. New York: Routledge.

Bornstein, K. (1998). *My gender workbook*. New York: Routledge.

Brown, L. M. (2005). In the bad or good of girlhood: Social class, schooling, and white femininities. In L. Weis & M. Fine (Eds.), *Beyond silenced voices: Class, race, and gender in United States schools* (Rev. ed., pp. 147–162). Albany, NY: State University of New York Press.

Califia, P. (1997). *Sex changes: The politics of transgenderism*. San Francisco: Cleis Press.

Chase, C. (2003). Hermaphrodites with attitude: Mapping the emergence of intersex political activism. In R. J. Corber & S. Valocchi (Eds.), *Queer studies: An interdisciplinary reader* (pp. 31–45). Malden, MA: Blackwell.

Connell, R. W. (1995). *Masculinities*. Sydney: Allen and Unwin.

Cromwell, J. (1997). Traditions of gender diversity and sexualities: A female-to-male transgendered perspective. In S.-E. Jacobs, W. Thomas & S. Lang (Eds.), *Two-spirit people: Native American gender identity, sexuality, and spirituality* (pp. 119–142). Chicago, IL: University of Illinois Press.

De Beauvoir, S. (1949). *Le Deuxième Sexe* (108e ed.). Paris: Gallimard.

DSM-IV-TR Diagnostic Criteria For Gender Identity Disorder. (2003). *Psychiatric News, 38*(14), 32.

Fausto-Sterling, A. (1993). The five sexes: Why male and female are not enough. *The Sciences (March-April)*, 20–24.

Fausto-Sterling, A. (2000). *Sexing the body: Gender politics and the construction of sexuality*. New York: Basic Books.

Feinberg, L. (1998). Allow me to introduce myself. In *Transliberation: Beyond pink or blue*. Boston, MA: Beacon Press.

GIRES. (2006). Atypical gender identity development – A review. *International Journal of Transgenderism, 9*(1), 29–44.

Hart, J. (2003, September 21). United genders of the Universe. Retrieved October 17, 2007, from http://unitedgenders.org/index.html

Hausman, K. (2003). Controversy continues to grow over DSM's GID Diagnosis. *Psychiatric News, 38*(14), 25–32.

Kehoe, A. (1997). On the Incommensurability of gender categories. In S.-E. Jacobs, W. Thomas & S. Lang (Eds.), *Two-spirit people: Native American gender identity, sexuality, and spirituality* (pp. 265–271). Chicago, IL: University of Illinois Press.

Kohlberg, L. (1966). A cognitive-developmental analysis of children's sex-role concepts and attitudes. In E. E. Maccoby (Ed.), *The development of sex differences* (pp. 82–172). Stanford, CA: Stanford University Press.

Lang, S. (1997). Various kinds of two-spirit people: Gender variance and homosexuality in Native American communities. In S.-E. Jacobs, W. Thomas & S. Lang (Eds.), *Two-spirit people: Native American gender identity, sexuality, and spirituality* (pp. 100–118). Chicago: University of Illinois.

Mac an Ghaill, M. (1995). *The making of men: Masculinities, sexualities, and schooling.* Philadelphia, PA: Open University Press.

Meyer, E. J. (2006). Gendered harassment in North America: School-based interventions for reducing homophobia and heterosexism. In C. Mitchell & F. Leach (Eds.), *Combating gender violence in and around schools* (pp. 43–50). Stoke on trent, UK: Trentham Books.

Mills, M. (2001). *Challenging violence in schools: An issue of masculinities.* Buckingham: Open University Press.

Money, J. (1973). Gender role, gender identity, core gender identity: Usage and definition of terms. *Journal of American Academy of Psychoanalysis, 1,* 397–402.

Nestle, J., Howell, C., & Wilchins, R. (Eds.). (2002). *Gender queer. Voices from beyond the sexual binary.* New York: Alyson Books.

O'Connor, C., Lewis, R. L. H., & Mueller, J. (2005). The culture of black femininity and school success. In L. Weis & M. Fine (Eds.), *Beyond silenced voices: Class, race, and gender in United States schools* (pp. 163–180). Albany, NY: State University of New York Press.

Pollack, W. (2002). Real Boys: The truths behind the myths. In *The Jossey-Bass reader on gender in education* (pp. 88–100). San Francisco: Jossey-Bass.

Preves, S. (2009). Intersex narratives: Gender, medicine, and identity. In A. L. Ferber, K. Holcomb & T. Wentling (Eds.), *Sex, gender, & sexuality: The new basics* (pp. 32–42). New York: Oxford University Press.

Rubin, G. (1975). The traffic in women: Notes on the 'Political Economy' of sex. In R. R. Reiter (Ed.), *Toward and anthropology of women* (pp. 157–210). New York and London: Monthly Review Press.

Rubin, G. (1984/1993). Thinking sex: Notes for a radical theory of the politics of sexuality. In H. Abelove, M. A. Barale & D. M. Halperin (Eds.), *The Lesbian and gay studies reader* (pp. 3–44). New York: Routledge.

Sax, L. (2005). *Why gender matters: What parents and teachers need to know about the emerging science of sex differences.* New York: Broadway Books.

Smith, B. (2007). *The psychology of sex and gender.* Boston, MA: Pearson.

Smith, Y. L. S., Van Goozen, S. H. M., & Cohen-Kettenis, P. T. (2001). Adolescents With gender identity disorder who were accepted or rejected for sex reassignment surgery: A prospective follow-up study. *Journal of the American Academy of Child & Adolescent Psychiatry, 40*(4), 472–481.

Sullivan, N. (2003). *A critical introduction to queer theory.* New York: New York University Press.

Tucker, D. (Writer) (2005). Transamerica [film]. New York: Belladonna Productions.

Wilchins, R. A. (1997). Lines in the sand, cries of desire. In C. Queen & L. Schimel (Eds.), *Pomosexuals: Challenging assumptions about gender and sexuality* (pp. 138–149). San Francisco: Cleis Press.

Chapter 3
Understanding Sexuality

Myths and misconceptions about sexuality:
(1) Sexuality refers only to sexual behaviors.
(2) Sexual orientation develops after puberty.
(3) Sexuality is determined by one's sex.
(4) There are professionally endorsed therapies that can permanently change a person's sexual orientation.

3.1 Introduction

Sexuality: it is a hot topic sure to spark controversy in any school community. Most teachers and administrators avoid the issue at all costs. Many parents also avoid the issue with their children due to their own discomfort. This absence of adult support leaves many young people without guidance and accurate information about relationships, physical development, sexual health, and important aspects of their identities. It also creates a school environment that is hostile for students who don't conform to the heterosexual social hierarchies of the school. This non-conformity can be for a wide variety of reasons: clothes, hairstyle, body size, makeup and accessories (too much, not enough, the "wrong" kind), and extracurricular interests. These behaviors are often connected to perceptions of a student's masculinity, femininity, or sexual orientation and often results in a student being excluded and/or targeted for bullying and harassment (California Safe Schools Coalition, 2004; Kosciw & Diaz, 2006; Meyer, 2006).

One of the most important things to remember when talking about sexuality is that everybody has one. Heterosexual, bisexual, gay, lesbian, queer, and asexual are some of the descriptors used when talking about sexuality. A person's sexuality and associated sexual identity intersects and interacts with other identities we may have such as gender, ethnic, class, dis/ability, racialized, and religious.

This chapter discusses important factors related to addressing sexual diversity in schools and begins by defining sexual diversity and several related terms that are important for education professionals to understand. The second section explores contemporary youth sexualities and some of the various identities embraced by

E.J. Meyer, *Gender and Sexual Diversity in Schools*, Explorations of Educational Purpose 10, DOI 10.1007/978-90-481-8559-7_3, © Springer Science+Business Media B.V. 2010

youth today. The next section gives a brief history of the stigma around sexualities in Western cultures and how this has been reflected in the institution of the school. Finally, the chapter will conclude by explaining the importance of having education professionals be able to address issues relating to sexual orientation accurately and sensitively.

3.2 What Is Sexuality?

Sexuality is a term that is used to refer to an individual's tendencies, preferences, and desires with respect to romantic partners and intimate relationships. Sometimes sexual orientation is used interchangeably with the term sexuality; however, sexuality can be used more broadly to refer to a wide variety of identities and behaviors as well. Since this book is written for the current or future professional educator, the focus will be on everyday issues that are already present in schools. We cannot separate ourselves from our identities and how our orientations influence these identities, nor can we ask students to do so. Therefore, identity and orientation will be the focus of this chapter, not behavior. This is an important distinction to make since most controversies surrounding school efforts to be more supportive of sexual diversity result from opponents mistakenly believing that explicit details of sexual behavior will be taught and discussed. This is generally not true. With the exception of some officially approved sexuality education programs, most initiatives on sexual diversity specifically address issues of respect, physical and emotional safety, friendships, family dynamics, and identity as well as the harmful impacts of inaccurate myths, stereotypes, discriminatory attitudes, and behaviors. There are four important terms that must be carefully explained to help educators understand various elements related to sexual diversity: *sexuality, sexual orientation, sexual behavior,* and *sexual identity.*

3.2.1 Sexuality

Sexuality is a term that has different meanings depending on the context of its use. As mentioned above, every person has a sexuality and this is often used to describe a range of internal identities and external behaviors. Many individuals have not reflected on their own sexuality because it has not caused them tension or struggle in their lives. However, many others have learned to be more aware of their sexualities as a result of exclusion or discrimination they may have experienced as a result of how their tendencies, predispositions, and desires (orientation) have impacted their sense of themselves (identity) and how they interact with others (behavior) (Blumenfeld, 1994). Each of these terms are explained in more detail below.

3.2.2 Sexual Orientation

Sexual orientation describes who we are sexually attracted to and is generally de
mined at a very young age. The four main categories of sexual orientation include
the following:

(1) *asexuals* – not attracted to people of any sex
(2) *bi-/omni-/pansexuals* – attracted to some members of both/all sexes to varying
    degrees
(3) *heterosexuals* – primarily attracted to some members of another sex
(4) *homosexuals* – primarily attracted to some persons of the same sex

Scholars disagree on whether sexual orientation is determined by biology,
including genes and hormones, or sociology, mostly influenced by upbringing and
environment. However, most researchers acknowledge that it is a result of the interaction of the two (Lipkin, 1999, pp. 25–28). Regardless of which factor exerts a
larger force on one's sexual orientation, there is general agreement that sexual orientation is decided early in a child's life and cannot be changed. For example,
one study found that gay, lesbian, and bisexual (GLB) youth report first becoming aware of their sexual orientation at age ten (D'Augelli & Hershberger, 1993)
and another reported that gay adolescents report becoming aware of a distinct feeling of "being different" between ages 5 and 7 (Leo & Yoakum, 1992). Although
there are some medical professionals and religious groups that claim to be able
to change a person's sexual orientation, professional organizations including The
American Academy of Pediatrics, The American Counseling Association, The
American Psychiatric Association, The American Psychological Association, and
The National Association of Social Workers do not endorse any form of counseling that is some form of "reparative therapy" or secks to change a person's sexual
orientation (Frankfurt, 1999).

3.2.3 Sexual Behavior

Sexual behavior is a term used to describe the types of sexual activities an individual actually engages in. There is a wide array of sexual behaviors people may
engage in depending on what arouses them physically and emotionally. It is important to acknowledge that the sex of one's partner does not limit the types of sexual
behaviors one can engage in. One can find as much diversity of sexual behaviors
within a group of heterosexuals as there is between heterosexuals, bisexuals, and
homosexuals. For example, in the late 1940s and early 1950s Alfred Kinsey and his
colleagues conducted a series of interviews with men and women about their sexual
desires and behaviors. In this study, they found the participants engaged in many
types of sexual behaviors regardless of the sex of their partners. He also noted that

approximately 37% of adult males and 19% of adult females have had some same-sex erotic experience to the point of orgasm. In his report he noted that this number was most likely artificially low due to reluctance of participants to disclose about same-sex behaviors (Kinsey, Pomeroy, & Martin, 1948, p. 623; Kinsey, Pomeroy, Martin, & Gebhard, 1953, p. 453).

Sexual behavior is generally informed by one's sexual orientation, but not always. Since behavior can be chosen, people may choose to engage in certain behaviors and not others. These can also be influenced by one's culture, social group, and romantic partners. It is not uncommon for people who feel attracted to members of the same sex to engage in heterosexual relationships to avoid stigmatization and isolation from friends if they were to "come out" as gay or lesbian, nor is it uncommon for heterosexuals to engage in some same-sex behaviors. Orientation influences our behavior; it does not dictate it. However when orientation and behavior are in conflict it is difficult for an individual to develop a cohesive sexual identity and a healthy sense of self (Cass, 1984; Troiden, 1988).

3.2.4 Sexual Identity

Sexual identity is how a person chooses to describe himself or herself. This can include cultural and political labels as well as other identifiers that may connect a person with a community and a commonality to others who share their chosen identity. The identity formation process can be long and complex and many theories exist that use stage models to describe this process for individuals in Western cultures including the works of Sigmund Freud, Erik Erikson, and Jean Piaget. More recently, scholars have developed theories of identity development that seek to explain the shared experiences of youth who identify as gay, lesbian, queer, or same-sex attracted (Cass, 1979, 1984; Dube & Savin-Williams, 1999; Kumashiro, 2001; Troiden, 1988). Although these theories explain some of the commonalities individuals may experience, it is important to acknowledge that this process is shaped and influenced by factors such as friends, school, class, race, ethnicity, religion, and gender identity and expression (Rowen & Malcolm, 2002; Waldner-Haugrud & Magruder, 1996). Some of the more widely recognized sexual identities embraced by contemporary youth are discussed at greater length in the next section.

3.3 Understanding Diverse Sexual Identities

In conversations of sexual orientation, the realities and experiences of heterosexual-identified, or straight, individuals are often ignored. This is a common error in diversity work where the focus is on the marginalized "other" rather than on understanding the perspective and experiences of those in the dominant group. It is important to discuss heterosexuality especially in terms of heterosexual privilege and how it works to make some people's relationships and experiences more valued than others. One valuable pedagogical tool available to help students explore heterosexual privilege is a short quiz called, "The Heterosexual Questionnaire." This activity was created by Martin Rochlin, Ph.D., in 1977 and has been adapted for use in anti-homophobia trainings around the world. Sample questions from this activity include the following:

(1) What do you think caused your heterosexuality?
(2) When and how did you first decide you were heterosexual?
(3) Is it possible that your heterosexuality is just a phase you may grow out of?
(4) If heterosexuality is normal, why are so many mental patients heterosexual?
(5) The great majority of child molesters are heterosexual males. Do you consider it safe to expose your children to heterosexual teachers?
(6) Would you want your children to be heterosexual, knowing the problems they would face, such as heartbreak, disease, and divorce? (Advocates for Youth, 2005)

These questions may then stimulate the reader to reflect on social assumptions about heterosexuality and the related stereotypes and stigmas attached to homosexuality. Although there can be controversy if this tool is not used in the proper context or the conversations are not well facilitated (Rasmussen, Mitchell, & Harwood, 2007), it often leads to a greater awareness on the part of heterosexuals with regard to how heteronormativity and heterosexism, also known as heterosexual privilege, function.

The terms "gay" and "lesbian" are the preferred terms to use when speaking about people who identify as homosexual. Although the term "homosexual" is widely used in the medical and psychological professional communities, it has a very specific history and meaning. When using the term "homosexual" these professional organizations are generally referring to individuals who engage exclusively in same-sex sexual behaviors. This does not necessarily mean that these individuals choose to identify as gay or lesbian. The term "gay" came into wider use to describe men who engage in same-sex relationships during the gay liberation movement that erupted after the famous police raid at The Stonewall Inn on June 27, 1969, in New York City (Jagose, 1996). Although the word "gay" can be used to describe women as well, many women prefer the term "lesbian." This word also has a political history attached to the women's liberation movement of the 1960s and 1970s and is often associated with the concept of lesbian-feminists. Some of these activists considered themselves separatists and chose to live and work independently and separate from men (Jagose, 1996). It is no mistake that these terms both gained wider use during this era of important political changes. The concept of identity politics asserts that "coming out" and publicly identifying as gay or lesbian was an important step to achieving public visibility, reducing negative stereotypes, and therefore securing greater social equality (Weeks, 1985). Due to the historical specificity and cultural stereotypes that have grown up around these terms, many individuals who engage in same-sex behaviors and relationships may choose to use different words to identify themselves.

For people who do not identify as heterosexual, the terms gay and lesbian are not the only ones they may choose to describe themselves. Many adolescents and young adults prefer terms such as bi-curious, fluid, hetero- or homo-flexible, open, omni-sexual, pan-sexual, polyamorous, questioning, or queer (Driver, 2007, pp. 42–43; Meyer, 2008). Although the term *queer* has changed over the years from meaning odd or strange to being an insult for gays and lesbians, it is now being reclaimed as a powerful political term by the gay, lesbian, bisexual, and transgender community (Jagose, 1996; Meyer, 2007). When used as a source of pride and with a sense of inclusivity, "queer" can be a very empowering term. However, if used to insult and exclude it still has the power to wound deeply. As Driver explains in her book *Queer girls and popular culture*, "queer as a strategically chosen term works against the foreclosure of desires and the imposition of controlling assumptions; it is deployed by girls as a way of enabling possibilities rather than guaranteeing identity or knowl-edge about identity" (Driver, 2007, p. 43). There are many individuals who reject static labels and choose not to identify their sexuality in any way. This demonstrates a move away from the identity politics of the gay and lesbian rights movement, and the postmodern tendency for young people to create new identities and communities that are fluid and shifting and more authentically represent their experiences.

All of these identity categories are complicated and formed over an individual's lifetime. Although some people argue that sexuality is an inappropriate topic to dis-cuss with younger children, their lives are impacted by sexual diversity. In addition to their own developing sense of themselves, they are influenced by the lives of the adults around them. Many educators who work in early childhood and elementary education believe that discussions of sexual diversity have no place in their schools. However, most families in Western cultures are based on relationships created out of romantic love; thus children's home lives and family structures tend to reflect the sexualities of their parents and caregivers. Recent studies on the experiences of children of gay and lesbian parents indicate that they experience increased harass-ment at school and their parents were often excluded from school life (Kosciw & Diaz, 2008; Ray & Gregory, 2001). For these reasons it is important for educa-tors to address diverse family structures and be inclusive of sexual diversity when addressing diversity issues with students of all ages. *It's Elementary: Talking about gay issues in* schools is an excellent film that provides models of how to do this appropriately and effectively with younger students (Chasnoff, 1996). In addition to developing a better understanding of sexual diversity and how it impacts individual's lives, it is important for educators to be aware of the myths and misconceptions sur-rounding sexual orientation and how various institutions, including the school, have worked to perpetuate homophobia and heterosexism.

3.4 The History of Homophobia and Heterosexism

Historically, Western cultures have constructed homosexuality as an illness, a deviance, and a sin. This negative bias was created through psychological research, religious ideologies, and the political and financial privileging of heterosexual monogamous family structures by the state through marriage. This bias has been disrupted and challenged by the gay rights movements that gained momentum in the 1960s and 1970s. Many authors have examined the social, historical, and political forces that have worked together to construct the idea of the homosexual and then demonize it (Bem, 1993; Foucault, 1980; Jagose, 1996; Sears, 1998; Weeks, 1985).

Foucault traced the birth of the modern idea of the "homosexual" to the 1870s to an article by Westphal on "contrary sexual sensations" (1980, p. 43). Although sexual practices labeled as "sodomy" had been criminalized in Europe as early as 1477 (Sullivan, 2003, p. 3), individuals who had engaged in such behaviors had never been categorized as a class of persons. As Foucault explains, "The sodomite had been a temporary aberration; the homosexual was now a species" (1980, p. 43). It was during the late 1800s that a public discourse around homosexuality emerged and lawyers (Karl Heinrich Ulrichs), psychiatrists (Richard von Krafft-Ebing, Sigmund Freud), and sexologists (Havelock Ellis, Carl Westphal, and Magnus Hirschfield) began to define the terms that were used to view homosexuality as a perversion, illness, pathology, or abnormality (Sullivan, 2003, p. 7). Although many of these men were working with the goal of reducing the persecution of (male) homosexuals, the terms in which they framed the debate were used to help justify the criminalization, medical treatment, and institutionalization of individuals identified as homosexual.

The main focus on male sexuality underlines the phallocentric construction of sexuality in Western European cultures, but Lillian Faderman examined the impacts of this work on women's lives in her work *Surpassing the Love of Men*. She asserts that before this time period, "romantic friendships" between women were socially sanctioned and it was the concurrent emergence of first-wave feminism in the early 1900s that produced this change in attitude. Faderman explains, "the sexologists' theories frightened, or attempted to frighten, women away from feminism and from loving other women by demonstrating that both were abnormal and were generally linked together" (cited in Jagose, 1996, p. 14). The emergence of the identity category "homosexual" during this era led to the new term "heterosexuality" to define opposite-sex identities. Without the exploration of same-sex desire and behavior, the dominant way of being, heterosexuality, had never been named or examined. The fact that heterosexuality was created to describe behaviors and identities that were not homosexual is an important fact to consider when examining issues related to sex, gender, and sexual orientation in contemporary Western society.

Heterosexism, compulsory heterosexuality (Rich, 1978/1993), the heterosexual matrix (Butler, 1990), and gender polarization (Bem, 1993) are all different terms that seek to explain the social construction of opposite-sex attraction and sexual behavior as dominant and "normal." The concept of homosexuality and subsequently heterosexuality is just over a century old (Jagose, 1996, p. 17). The resulting prejudice against those who deviate from the heterosexual social script has been carefully developed by institutional heterosexism through organized religion, medicine, sexology, psychiatry, and psychology (Bem, 1993, p. 81). Sandra

Bem explains how the cultural lens of *gender polarization* works to reinforce heterosexuality by serving two major functions:

> first, it defines mutually exclusive scripts for being male and female. Second, it defines any person or behaviour that deviates from these scripts as problematic... taken together, the effect of these two processes is to construct and naturalize a gender-polarizing link between the sex of one's body and the character of one's psyche and one's sexuality (1993, p. 81).

These powerful social discourses are generated through various institutions including schools. As Foucault argues, institutions contributed to the creation of multiple sexualities in their attempts to control and regulate them.

> Educational or psychiatric institutions, with their large populations, their hierarchies, their spatial arrangements, their surveillance systems, constituted, alongside the family, another way of distributing the interplay of powers and pleasures; but they too delineated areas of extreme sexual saturation, with privileged spaces or rituals such as the classroom, the dormitory, the visit, and the consultation. The forms of a nonconjugal, nonmonogamous sexuality were drawn there and established (1980, p. 46).

The ideological power of schools is significant due to their role in teaching what the culture has deemed as important and valuable to future generations.

Ministries of Education, textbook publishers, and teachers determine what lessons are passed on to students and whose knowledge or "truth" is valued (Apple, 1990, 2000). Subsequently, schools are important sites that contribute to the normalization of heterosexual behavior. In Richard Friend's article, *Choices not closets*, he exposes two ways that such lessons are passed on in schools through the processes of systematic inclusion and systematic exclusion. Systematic inclusion is the way in which negative or false information about homosexuality is introduced in schools as a pathology or deviant behavior. Systematic exclusion is "the process whereby positive role models, messages, and images about lesbian, gay and bisexual people are publicly silenced in schools" (Friend, 1993, p. 215). Ironically, schools make efforts to de-sexualize the experience of students while they simultaneously, subtly yet clearly, affirm heterosexual behaviors and punish those who appear to deviate from it. Epstein and Johnson explain,

> Schools go to great lengths to forbid expressions of sexuality by both children and teachers. This can be seen in a range of rules, particularly those about self-presentation. On the other hand, and perhaps in consequence, expressions of sexuality provide a major currency and resource in the everyday exchanges of school life. Second, the forms in which sexuality is present in schools and the terms on which sexual identities are produced are heavily determined by power relations between teachers and taught, the dynamics of control and resistance(1998, p. 108).

These acts of surveillance are rooted in Foucault's (1975) concept of the Panopticon – an all-seeing, yet completely invisible source of power and control. This type of surveillance and control is particularly effective because we all unknowingly contribute to it unless we actively work to make it visible by questioning and challenging it. This is one of the most powerful ways that schools reinforce heterosexism. Through the surveillance and policing of bodies and language, school structures mandate hyper-heterosexuality using the curriculum and extracurricular activities.

The heterosexuality of the curriculum is invisible to many due to its unquestioned dominance in schools and communities. Some examples include the exclusive study of heterosexual romantic literature, the presentation of the "nuclear" heterosexual two-parent family as the norm and ideal, and teaching only the reproductive aspects of sex or abstinence-only sex education. Other forms of relationships and the concept of desire, or *eros*, are completely omitted from the official curriculum (Britzman, 2000; Pinar, 1998). Extracurricular functions that also teach this compulsory heterosexuality include Valentine's Day gift exchanges, kissing booths at school fairs, and prom rituals that include highly gendered formal attire (tuxedos and gowns) and the election of a "king" and a "queen." This prom ritual has begun to be subverted by alternative proms often organized by gay–straight alliances or community youth groups. At these events there may be two kings (a male king and female "drag king") and two queens (a female queen and a male "drag queen").

Art Lipkin's (1999) groundbreaking work, *Understanding homosexuality, changing schools*, provides in-depth accounts of the discrimination experienced by gay, lesbian, and bisexual educators as well as the painful and enduring stories of students who were emotionally and physically harassed for their perceived or actual non-heterosexual, non-gender conforming performance of identity. In other words, schools are not safe for "guys who aren't as masculine as other guys" or "girls who aren't as feminine as other girls" (California Safe Schools Coalition, 2004). Although the people in control of the school are not directly inflicting the harassment and harm on the non-conforming students (in most cases), it is their lack of effective intervention in cases of homophobic and sexual harassment (Epstein & Johnson, 1998; Mac an Ghaill, 1995; Martino & Pallotta-Chiarolli, 2003) along with the invisible scripts of the school that are reinforced through surveillance and discipline that sends the message that these identities are not valued or welcomed.

Heterosexism and its more overt partner, homophobia, are clearly linked to cultural gender boundaries and are informed by misogyny. Misogyny is the hatred or devaluing of all that is female or "feminine." For example, the most effective challenge to any boy's masculinity is to call him "gay," "homo," "fag," or "queer" (Brown, 2003; Duncan, 2004). What is being challenged is his masculinity – his gender code – but it is being done by accusing him of being gay which is equated with being "feminine." Girls are also subject to similar kinds of policing, but research shows that it is much more prevalent among male students (Harris Interactive, 2001; California Safe Schools Coalition 2004). It is for this reason that some activists and educators are pushing for a deconstruction of gender codes and de-labeling of sexual orientations. By continuing to live within narrow boundaries of language and behavior, the hierarchical binaries of male–female and gay–straight remain unchallenged. This work of dismantling socially invented categories is necessary to create educational spaces that liberate and create opportunities as opposed to limiting and closing down the diversity of human experiences. We must move

ird understanding identities and experiences as falling on a continuum of gender
iressions and sexual orientations. Fortunately, there are many opportunities for
ucators to open up spaces in their classrooms and schools to support and value
sexual diversity.

3.5 Creating Schools That Value Sexual Diversity

While overt acts of discrimination are difficult for schools to ignore, daily acts of
covert discrimination persist and impact students' lives in ways that many teachers
and administrators fail to acknowledge. When bias against an identifiable social
group is present throughout an institution, the entire school is implicated and the
culture must shift. In order to transform ignorance of and intolerance for forms of
sexual diversity all stakeholders in the community must be involved in the process:
students, families, teachers, administrators, and school board personnel. The tone
must be set by the leadership, but everyone must be engaged in changing the culture
of the institution. Specific strategies for school change are addressed in greater depth
in Chapter 7. However, it is important to address why it is important for educators
to be supportive of sexual diversity within the existing structures of their school
for reasons of ensuring student safety, teaching human rights, and valuing family
diversity.

First, educators are responsible for the physical and emotional safety of the
students in their classroom and school. If they are not able to address forms of
discrimination and harassment appropriately, they will not be able to create this safe
and supportive learning environment.

Second, schools are given the responsibility of educating future leaders and
engaged citizens and must model the values and behaviors they seek to instill in
their students. Understanding and respecting human rights is an important aspect
of citizenship. In addition to teaching students essential academic skills, educators
cannot ignore the citizenship and interpersonal skills that students will also need as
they mature into adults.

Finally, with the changing demographics of modern society, the two-parent heterosexual nuclear family is more and more rare. In order to value the true diversity
in student's home lives and honestly explore the different family structures that exist
in North America, educators must be able to speak frankly and openly about love,
family, and relationships with their students.

In addition to developing a better understanding of sexual diversity and how it
impacts individual's lives, it is important for educators to be aware of the various
curricular, extracurricular, legal, and safety issues involved that relate to the topic
of sexual diversity in schools. These topics, along with suggestions for improving
school cultures are addressed in Part II of this book.

References

Advocates for Youth. (2005). The Heterosexual questionnaire. Retrieved March 2, 2008, from http://www.advocatesforyouth.org/lessonplans/heterosexual2.htm

Apple, M. (1990). *Ideology and the curriculum*. New York: Routledge.

Apple, M. (2000). *Official knowledge: Democratic education in a conservative age* (2nd ed.). New York: Routledge.

Bem, S. (1993). *The lenses of gender: Transforming the debate on sexual inequality*. New Haven, CT: Yale University Press.

Blumenfeld, W. (1994). Science, sexual orientation, and identity: An overview. Unpublished research paper. Gay, Lesbian, and Straight Education Network.

Britzman, D. (2000). Precocious education. In S. Talburt & S. Steinberg (Eds.), *Thinking queer: Sexuality, culture, and education* (pp. 33–60). New York: Peter Lang.

Brown, L. M. (2003). *Girlfighting: Betrayal and rejection among girls*. New York: New York University Press.

Butler, J. (1990). *Gender trouble*. New York: Routledge Falmer.

California Safe Schools Coalition. (2004). *Consequences of harassment based on actual or perceived sexual orientation and gender non-conformity and steps for making schools safer*. Davis: University of California.

Cass, V. (1979). Homosexual identity formation: A theoretical model. *Journal of Homosexuality*, 4, 219–235.

Cass, V. (1984). Homosexual identity formation: Testing a theoretical model. *The Journal of Sex Research*, 20, 143–167.

Chasnoff, D. (Writer) (1996). It's Elementary: Talking about gay issues in school. In H. S. Cohen & D. Chasnoff (Producer). San Francisco, CA: Ground Spark.

D'Augelli, A. R., & Hershberger, S. L. (1993). Lesbian, gay, and bisexual youth in community settings: Personal challenges and mental health problems. *American Journal of Community Psychology*, 21, 421–448.

Driver, S. (2007). *Queer girls and popular culture: Reading, resisting, and creating media*. New York: Peter Lang.

Dube, E., & Savin-Williams, R. (1999). Sexual identity development among ethnic sexual-minority male youths. *Developmental Psychology*, 35(6), 1389–1398.

Duncan, N. (2004). It's important to be nice, but it's nicer to be important: Girls, popularity and sexual competition. *Sex Education*, 4(2), 137–152.

Epstein, D., & Johnson, R. (1998). *Schooling sexualities*. Buckingham: Open University Press.

Foucault, M. (1975). *Surveiller et Punir: Naissance de la Prison*. Paris: Gallimard.

Foucault, M. (1980). *The History of sexuality, Vol. I: An introduction*. New York: Random House.

Frankfurt, K. (1999). *Just the facts about sexual orientation and youth: A primer for principals, educators, and school personnel*. New York: GLSEN, National Education Association, American Psychological Association, American Federation of Teachers, the National Association of School Psychologists, and the National Association of Social Workers.

Friend, R. (1993). Choices, not closets: Heterosexism and homophobia in schools. In L. Weis & M. Fine (Eds.), *Beyond silenced voices: Class, race, and gender in United States schools* (pp. 209–235). Albany, NY: State University of New York Press.

Harris Interactive. (2001). *Hostile hallways: Bullying, teasing, and sexual harassment in school*. Washington, DC: American Association of University Women Educational Foundation.

Jagose, A. (1996). *Queer theory: An introduction*. New York: New York University Press.

Kinsey, A., Pomeroy, W., & Martin, C. (1948). *Sexual behavior in the human male*. Philadelphia, PA: W.B. Saunders Company.

Kinsey, A., Pomeroy, W., Martin, C., & Gebhard, P. (1953). *Sexual behavior in the human female*. Philadelphia, PA: W.B. Saunders Co.

Kosciw, J., & Diaz, E. (2006). *The 2005 national school climate survey: The experiences of lesbian, gay, bisexual and transgender youth in our nation's schools*. New York: The Gay, Lesbian and Straight Education Network.

Kosciw, J., & Diaz, E. (2008). *Involved, invisible, ignored: The experiences of lesbian, gay, bisexual and transgender parents and their children in our Nation's K–12 schools*. New York: GLSEN.

Kumashiro, K. K. (Ed.). (2001). *Troubling intersections of race and sexuality: Queer students of color and anti-oppressive education*. Lanham, MD: Rowman & Littlefield.

Leo, T., & Yoakum, J. (1992). Creating a safer school environment for lesbian and gay students *Journal of school health (September)*, 37–41.

Lipkin, A. (1999). *Understanding homosexuality, Changing schools*. Boulder, CO: Westview Press.

Mac an Ghaill, M. (1995). *The making of men: Masculinities, sexualities, and schooling*. Philadelphia, PA: Open University Press.

Martino, W., & Pallotta-Chiarolli, M. (2003). *So what's a boy? Addressing issues of masculinity and schooling*. Buckingham: Open University Press.

Meyer, E. J. (2006). Gendered harassment in North America: School-based interventions for reducing homophobia and heterosexism. In C. Mitchell & F. Leach (Eds.), *Combating gender violence in and around schools* (pp. 43–50). Stoke on Trent: Trentham Books.

Meyer, E. J. (2007). But I'm not gay: What straight teachers need to know about queer theory. In N. Rodriguez & W. F. Pinar (Eds.), *Queering straight teachers* (pp. 1–17). New York: Peter Lang.

Meyer, E. J. (2008). Lesbians in popular culture. In C. Mitchell & J. Reid-Walsh (Eds.), *Girl culture: an encyclopedia* (Vol. 2, pp. 392–394). Westport, CT: Greenwood Press.

Pinar, W. F. (1998). Understanding curriculum as gender text: Notes on reproduction, resistance, and male-male relations. In M. M. William F. Pinar, M. A. Doll (Ed.), *Queer theory in education*. Mahwah, NJ: Lawrence Erlbaum Associates.

Rasmussen, M. L., Mitchell, J., & Harwood, V. (2007). The queer story of The Heterosexual Questionnaire. In N. Rodriguez & W. F. Pinar (Eds.), *Queering straight teachers: Discourse and identity in education* (pp. 95–112). New York: Peter Lang.

Ray, V., & Gregory, R. (2001). School experiences of the children of lesbian and gay parents. *Family matters*, 59, 28–34.

Rich, A. (1978/1993). Compulsory heterosexuality and lesbian existence. In H. Abelove, D. Halperin & M. A. Barale (Eds.), *The lesbian and gay studies reader* (pp. 227–254). New York: Routledge.

Rowen, C. J., & Malcolm, J. P. (2002). Correlates of internalized homophobia and homosexual identity formation in a sample of gay men. *Journal of Homosexuality*, 43(2), 77–92.

Sears, J. T. (1998). A generational and theoretical analysis of culture and male (Homo)sexuality. In W. F. Pinar (Ed.), *Queer theory in education* (pp. 73–105). Mahwah, NJ: Lawrence Erlbaum and Associates.

Sullivan, N. (2003). *A Critical introduction to queer theory*. New York: New York University Press.

Troiden, R. R. (1988). The formation of homosexual identities. *Journal of Homosexuality*, 17(1/2), 43–74.

Waldner-Haugrud, L., & Magruder, B. (1996). Homosexual identity expression among lesbian and gay adolescents: An analysis of perceived structural associations. *Youth and Society*, 27(3), 313–333.

Weeks, J. (1985). *Sexuality and its discontents*. New York: Routledge.

Part II
Experiencing Gender and Sexual Diversity in Schools

Chapter 4
Integrating Gender and Sexual Diversity Across the Curriculum

Myths and misconceptions about teaching about sexual and gender diversity:
(1) When talking about sexual or gender diversity, educators will have to speak explicitly about sexual behaviors.
(2) Issues relating to gender and sexuality are exclusively private matters and should only be discussed in the home.
(3) Teaching about gender and sexual diversity may contradict certain religious beliefs; therefore it does not belong in public school curriculum.
(4) It is not my job to teach this since diversity issues are not relevant to my subject area.

4.1 Introduction

Due to the perceived controversial nature of gender and sexuality topics in schools, many educators may feel discomfort or resistance to the idea of integrating issues related to gender and sexual diversity into the formal curriculum of the school. Community members who are resistant to including these topics in schools present counter-arguments that explain that the subject matter is too controversial or that parents' have rights to be the sole source of information on these topics for their children, as well as using faith-based arguments that support excluding any form of sexuality education in public schools.

However, what most families and educators do not realize is that there is already a very powerful hidden curriculum that is teaching very narrow and restrictive lessons to students about sex and gender as well as what sexualities are valued at school, and by extension, society as a whole. This hidden curriculum (Apple, 2000) is shaped by jokes and comments made informally between students and among school staff, by what relationships are allowed to be discussed openly in the lunchroom and between classes, by school-sanctioned social events such as dances and Valentine's Day gift exchanges, and what sports and activities are supported for girls and boys in that community. While never named, heterosexuality and heteronormativity is reinforced through all of these practices and school experiences. Public schools were created to support the needs and interests of all children in a democratic society including gay, lesbian, and bisexual youth, children of BGLQT parents, transgender youth, and youth who may have non-normative interests for their sex. In order to create safe spaces for everyone in schools, teachers, administrators, and other youth workers should proactively demystify issues of gender and sexual diversity and teach toward acceptance and valuing of these differences.

In order to help educators apply the information presented in the first part of this book, this chapter offers concrete suggestions for teachers in elementary and secondary schools on how to integrate lessons regarding gender and sexual diversity into their existing curricula. It is important to situate these pedagogical approaches into existing approaches to teaching, so the first section of this chapter is dedicated to showing these links. The seven main schools of thought outlined in Chapter 1 have different names and subtle theoretical nuances in language and scholarship, but they have more similarities than differences when it comes to practical application in the classroom. Each of these philosophies has the explicit intent of improving the quality of life for all members of a democratic society. These approaches propose that equality and social justice can be achieved by promoting critical thinking and a high level of intellectual and social engagement through carefully structured classroom activities. Although the structure and content of these methods will vary by age and subject matter, there are some common themes that can be applied by any teacher in any classroom environment. Although there may be some resistance to the inclusion of these topics in the classroom, it is important to reiterate that issues of gender and sexuality are already prevalent in schools. It is only a matter of deciding whose perspectives and whose identities and relationships are allowed to be included in these conversations.

This section of the chapter is broken down into three parts: approaches to teaching, elementary topics and themes, and secondary topics and themes. The first part introduces some teaching methods that can be applied in any classroom context in order to support the aforementioned pedagogical approaches. The second part outlines some common areas covered in elementary curriculum where topics related to gender and sexual diversity can be easily integrated. The third part focuses on themes and topics commonly covered in secondary curricular areas where lessons and activities related to gender and sexual diversity may be taught.

4.2 Approaches to Teaching

In order to create a school or classroom environment that is a safe space where multiple perspectives and ideas are encouraged and valued, teachers must work explicitly and consistently to meet this goal. Students should be encouraged to talk through their differences with adult support and learn from their divergent points of view. Teachers should establish basic expectations early in the school year through a classroom contract or code of conduct that is co-constructed with the students in the class so they feel ownership over the support and reinforcement of the rules or guidelines. By establishing clear expectations for behavior and participation early on and in a collective way, teachers not only model the behaviors they seek to develop in their students, but they engage them in a collective classroom activity that allows them to play a central role in creating the classroom community that they will be learning in year long. This is an example of a constructivist, or student-centered, learning activity.

Constructivist models of education are gaining in popularity across North America (DeVries, Zan, Hildebrandt, Edmiaston, & Sales, 2001; Steffe & Gale, 1995). Constructivist pedagogy places the students at the center of the learning process and actively engages them in ways that more traditional, didactic teaching methods cannot. Classroom activities that encourage the students to ask questions, pursue their own interests, and work at their own pace all fit the constructivist model of teaching. Often teachers will lead the class in project-based learning that allows the students to discover answers on their own and teach each other along the way. Teachers can also introduce inquiry-based activities that allow students to work individually or in small groups to learn about a particular issue or problem and then share their knowledge with the rest of the class. This approach allows students to bring in new sources of information and allows multiple perspectives to be heard. Rather than students listening to the teacher or reading from a text book they are able to interview their families and community members, read books, and conduct searches in the library and on the Internet for additional sources of information. With the careful guidance of the teacher, students learn to evaluate various sources of information and make informed decisions about the perspectives that make the most sense in the context of what they are learning. These inquiry and critical thinking skills are higher-order skills than those of memorization and repetition that are practiced in a more traditional teacher-centered classroom.

A second approach to teaching that can allow the effective introduction of issues related to gender and sexual diversity in the classroom is democratic or citizenship education. These styles of teaching create a classroom environment that allows students to experience the democratic decision-making process. Just as the first example of creating a classroom contract demonstrates, it encourages students to share their ideas, debate the ones that evoke some controversy, and arrive at a decision that the entire class can live with. Democratic education isn't just about voting and "majority rules." It is about participating in the process and being given the opportunity to frame the debate and have one's own perspectives considered by others. Structured debates are one effective approach to discussing controversial issues in a class, school, or town community. Activities where students are encouraged to look at issues from multiple viewpoints and take a stand to defend a perspective on an issue can allow important learning to occur: not just on a particular subject, but on the process of learning and engaging in political processes.

Another citizenship activity can involve getting students involved in local political issues such as environmental pollution, housing, or a school reform. Supporting students' engagement on real-life problems that impact their communities can contribute to students' lifelong learning in ways that studying an issue in a textbook cannot. Teachers can suggest activities such as letter-writing campaigns, drafting and circulating petitions, attending school board and city council meetings, or planning and participating in a public demonstration. Although many teachers may shy away from such political involvement, there are compelling reasons to support such work with students. First, if the students choose the topic and the activities, then the project will engage them personally and reflect their interests and perspectives. Second, students often complain that what they are learning in school has no connection to real life and this is one way to address that concern. Third, as mentioned above, when students are asked to generate their own ideas, carefully evaluate the ideas of others, and construct an appropriate and reasoned response, they are using much more advanced academic skills than the ones they are called on to use in a more typical classroom environment. There are many stories of students using such skills to advocate for a gay–straight alliance in their school (*East High GSA v. Salt Lake City Board of Education*, 1999; Griffin, Lee, Waugh, & Beyer, 2004; Macgillivray, 2005; Mayo, 2004b), to plan a "Day of Silence" (*Harper v. Poway Unified School District*, 2006; Skowronski, 2008, April 3), or to take an organized stand against bullies in their school community by coordinating a "wear pink day" (Mills, 2007). Also, engaging in real-life work demonstrates intersectionality – that gender and sexual diversity issues are always connected to other communities' struggles for justice.

A third approach to teaching involves engaging students in a form of research called auto-ethnography, or self-study. This approach encourages participants to carefully examine their own identities and community affiliations as well as the privileges and biases that accompany them: what is valued and what is not in one's own family, school, or religious institution. This kind of teaching asks teachers and students to engage in reflective identity-work, much like that which was illustrated in the film *Freedom Writers* (LaGravenese, 2006). It asks students to "analyze their own lives in order to develop their practical consciousness about real injustices in society and to develop constructive responses" (Sleeter & Grant, 1994, p. 225). Although this approach might seem more appropriate at the secondary level, it can be done with younger students in different ways using visual arts, drama, storytelling, and other media to help students articulate their stories and perspectives. Some excellent examples of this are displayed in the film *Its elementary: Talking about gay issues in school* (Chasnoff, 1996). The next section provides more specific examples of how to address gender and sexual diversity in the elementary curriculum.

4.3 Elementary Topics and Themes

Many parents and professional educators do not immediately see the relevance of issues of gender and sexual diversity in elementary school classrooms. Unfortunately, many of these critics incorrectly believe that talking about diverse sexualities mean that there will be explicit conversations about sexual behaviors. In elementary schools, this is generally not age-appropriate, nor is it recommended. Issues of gender and sexual diversity affect everyone and do not only impact students after they have reached puberty. The two main issues of gender and sexual diversity that are most relevant in the lives of young children are those related to gender role expectations and parenting and family relationships.

4.3.1 Gender Roles

Gender roles are taught at school. When children enter pre-school and kindergarten they are learning much about gender codes and what is expected of them if they are a boy or a girl. They are often fixated on "what boys do" and "what girls wear" and most try very hard to follow these rules. Mindy Blaise, in her book *Playing it straight: Uncovering gender discourses in the early childhood classroom*, explains,

> It is clear that young children take an active part in the social construction of gender. Not only do children understand gender discourses, but they are also capable of accessing them in order to regulate gender in their everyday lives. Young children and the gender discourses they take part in are not determined exclusively by biological factors, nor are they only a consequence of being socialized into particular ways of being; rather they are a result of how children make sense of and enact gender discourses every day (Blaise, 2005, p. 183).

It is also quite normal for children who are male to have interests in stereotypically "girl" activities and vice versa; however many parents and teachers try to steer their children away from these atypical interests. These adults who consistently shape and mold children's behavior often do so in hopes of protecting the child from bullying, ridicule, or social exclusion. The problem with this approach is that it reinforces existing gender stereotypes that can deprive children of the opportunities to read books, engage in play activities, and pursue friendships that they truly enjoy. This fear of having boys act too girlish, and as a result, possibly be perceived as gay shows how homophobia is a by-product of sexism (Meyer, 2006; Pharr, 1988). As Chapter 2 indicated, there is much debate over whether one's gender identity and behavior are socially or biologically created; however there is much agreement that gender emerges very early in a child's life and efforts to influence or change it can have long-term negative consequences. In order to help students feel valued and included in all of their gender diversity, elementary school teachers can incorporate lessons and activities that celebrate this diversity and challenge narrow gender stereotypes. Some suggestions include

(1) When teaching about careers be sure to have images and role models that show men and women in a variety of career roles. If using photographs, try to use images that show a wide array of gender expressions.
(2) Be sure your class library and play centers include books and toys for all interests that aren't labeled or segregated by gender.
(3) Avoid having your students line up by sex: try using other organizing categories such as first name, last name, height, or birth month.
(4) When talking about families and home life, be sure to talk about the various roles and responsibilities that parents may have. Avoid talking about what "mommies do" and "daddies do" – especially since many students may have only one parent, or may be living with a grandparent or other caregiver.
(5) When choosing stories to read in class make sure you have a wide selection of stories that have girls and boys as main characters and that show girls as lead characters and show boys as caring and supportive friends. When reading such stories ask students questions about what the characters are doing and include

discussions about "boy things" and "girl things" if that matters to the children in the story.
(6) When choosing diverse representations of gender and sexuality in stories and images, pay attention to including people from different racial and ethnic backgrounds.

For additional suggestions and further reading on this topic, Mindy Blaise's *Playing it straight!: Uncovering gender discourses in the early childhood classroom* (2005) is an excellent resource as well as *Invisible boundaries: Addressing sexualities equality in children's worlds* (2008) by Renee DePalma and Elizabeth Atkinson. A third helpful resource is Will Letts & James Sears' *Queering elementary education: Advancing the dialogue about sexualities in schooling* (1999). In this book James Sears writes, "those who teach queerly refuse to participate in the great sexual sorting machine called schooling wherein diminutive GI Joes and Barbies become star quarterbacks and prom queens, while the Linuses and Tinky Winkys become wallflowers or human doormats" (p. 5). In this collection, Bickmore outlines some central features of the elementary curriculum in the Canadian Province, Ontario, that has commonalities with many curricula across North America. She writes,

> Ontario children, like children in many other locales, are expected to describe animal reproduction by grade 3, to identify human relationship challenges and responsibilities by grade 4, and to discuss puberty and human reproduction biology by grades 5 and 6. Grade 8 emphasizes ethical decision making in relationships and the application of "living skills" to sexual matters. (1999, p. 19).

Bickmore clearly links curricular expectations with issues of gender and sexuality in the elementary curriculum. In addition to understanding and learning about gender roles, topics related to parenting and loving family relationships are central to elementary school curricula and provide useful entry points for raising BGLQT visibility.

4.3.2 Parenting and Family Relationships

According to the National Adoption Information Clearinghouse, there are approximately 6–14 million children living with gay, lesbian, or bisexual parents in the United States and same-sex couples raising children live in 96% of all counties in the United States (COLAGE, 2009). In order for these children and families to feel welcomed and supported in their school communities, it is important for teachers to provide accurate and positive information about parenting and diverse family relationships. Theresa Bouley (2007) asserts, "In our efforts to provide the best learning environment possible for all children, we must break the silence, bring visibility to all families, and open up the discourse relating to the inclusion of gay/lesbian issues in elementary schools" (p. 141). One of the best ways to do this is through children's literature. Although most elementary teachers have a deep knowledge of some children's literature, research indicates that few can name even one book that depicts same-sex families (Bouley, 2007). Additionally, many teachers fear backlash from parents, administrators, and other community members. A powerful case study of such an event happened in a kindergarten classroom in British Columbia. James Chamberlain, a teacher who had students of same-sex parents in his classroom, attempted to introduce to his class three books that included same-sex families: *Asha's mums*, *Belinda's Bouquet*, and *One dad, two dads, brown dad, blue dad* (*Chamberlain v. Surrey School District No. 36*, 2002). His school district refused his request to add these books to his curriculum. He appealed their decision all the way to the Supreme Court of Canada which required that the school district lift the ban and reconsider its response. Mr. Chamberlain was finally successful in introducing similarly themed texts into his classroom. Being informed of local school policies and one's legal rights and responsibilities is one important strategy to help teachers best support all of their students. It is also helpful for educators to be aware of any union protections, or other labor practices that may be relevant in their district.

Fortunately, many educators and BGLQT advocacy organizations have compiled detailed reading lists of classroom resources that provide a positive and well-rounded depiction of same-sex families and children's experiences in those families. A few of the more popular titles include *And Tango makes three* (Richardson & Parnell, 2005), *Daddy's roommate* (Willhoite, 1990), *Heather has two mommies* (Newman, 2000), *King and king* (De Haan & Nijland, 2000), *The sissy duckling* (Fierstein, 2002), and *Williams' Doll* (Zolotow, 1972). For a more comprehensive list, please consult one of the following resources: *"Unleashing the unpopular"* (Killoran & Jimenez, 2007), *Challenging silence, challenging censorship* (Schrader & Wells, 2007), or GLSEN's online booklink (www.glsen.org/booklink). Incorporating issues of gender and sexual diversity in the elementary curriculum is not easy due to the limited awareness many teachers have of resources available for working with very young children. In 2009 The Human Rights Campaign released a new curriculum package called *Welcoming Schools* that offers a whole-school approach to teaching about many kinds of diversity in schools and it does a particularly good job at offering guidance and tangible suggestions for how to talk about gender and sexual diversity in elementary schools. This resource is available at www.hrc.org/weclomingschools. Classroom applications at the secondary level offer more in-depth opportunities, resources, and models to assist teachers interested in integrating these concepts into their classroom curricula.

4.4 Secondary Topics and Themes

Students in secondary schools are presented with a wide array of curricular content that can easily be adapted to include issues relating to gender and sexual diversity. Recent research indicates that incorporating BGLQT issues in a school's curriculum promotes feelings of safety and inclusiveness for all students in school (Kosciw, Diaz, & Gretytak, 2008; Russell, Kostroski, McGuire, Laub, & Manke 2006). However only 12% of students surveyed in a recent U.S. study ($n = 6191$) reported ever being taught about LGBT-related topics in school (Kosciw et al., 2008, p. 100). The most common courses where such topics were included when taught were History, English, and Health. Although courses in the humanities may seem more adaptable to discussions about gender and sexual diversity, there are also important lessons and content that can be included in Arts, Math, and Science courses as well. This section aims to provide some guidance for teachers interested in integrating these topics into their secondary curriculum.

4.4.1 English-Language Arts

The ability of the Language Arts curriculum to address a wide variety of subject matter allows a diverse range of topics and concerns to be discussed in these classes. Whether it be through students' stories, spoken word poetry, or the study of novels; Language Arts teachers can connect their students to multiple perspectives, experiences, and emotions through the curriculum. By assigning short stories, novels, poetry, and other texts that expose readers to different family structures, gender identities and expressions, and relationships, teachers can open up spaces for conversations and learning around gender and sexual diversity issues. Scholars have written about various texts to use and approaches to language arts teaching that can promote understandings of gender and sexual diversity (Blackburn, 2002; Blackburn & Buckley, 2005; Lipkin, 1995) and how to read or teach any text more critically (Kumashiro, 2004).

In middle grades (Grades 6–9) there are some wonderful books with accompanying lesson plans that support the discussion of respect for differences, including sexual orientation and gender identity such as *The Revealers* by Doug Wilhelm (lesson plan at http://www.adl.org/education/curriculum_connections), *The Misfits* by James Howe (lesson plans at www.nonamecallingweek.org), and *Luna* by Julie Ann Peters (lesson plans at http://www.hachettebookgroup.com/books_reading-group-guides.aspx). *The Revealers* and *The Misfits* both explore issues of friendship and respect for differences, and can be great approaches to dealing with issues of bullying and harassment in schools. *Luna* is a novel about a child who has a transgender sibling and explores issues of sibling relationships, family dynamics, as well as gender and identity themes.

Many high school courses read Shakespeare's *Romeo & Juliet* along with other novels and poetry that talk about heterosexual romantic love. One creative teacher has talked about alternative readings of this canonical text and how it can be used to explore forbidden relationships and the influence of family and community on adolescent relationships and identity formation (Ressler, 2005). She gives examples of exploring homoerotic and heteronormative excerpts of the text (Act 2, Scene 4, lines 15–95; Act 3, Scene 1, lines 11–120; and Act 3 Scene 3, lines 120–145) and discussed their meanings. She also discussed reframing the romance as a lesbian love story and examining Lady Capulet's reactions to the romance in that context (p. 55). Her examples infuse drama, role plays, reflective writing, and queer readings of this familiar text to help students go deeper into the multiple themes of this play and develop more critical literacy skills.

In addition to reading canonical texts through a queer lens, it would also be important to balance these representations with other stories and poems that have BGLQT subtexts and themes such as works by Walt Whitman, Edna St. Vincent

Millay, Langston Hughes, E.M. Forster, Willa Cather, Alice Walker, and Virginia Woolf. More recently, Jeffrey Eugenides' Pulitzer Prize-winning *Middlesex,* a novel about an intersex person, is another text that provides many opportunities to explore how sex, gender, and sexuality impact individuals' identities, experiences, relationships, and ways of being in the world. As Paula Ressler point out, "Reading queerly to explore nonnormative sex and gender identities, reading against a text that was written to deny equality to some, and reading for social justice and the creating of a better world have the potential to include all students in meaningful dialogue and to create engaged and successful learners and caring school communities" (p. 56). This would allow space for students to talk about different kinds of love and relationships and examine how they have been represented and experienced across history. This exposure may also open students' own creative lenses up and allow them to write about their own experiences in relationships or gendered identities in new ways.

4.4.2 History and Social Studies

The disciplines of History and Social Studies also lend themselves well to discussions of gender and sexual diversity. Just as many courses discuss important events such as the Holocaust, the Civil Rights Movement, and current events, these topics can easily be opened up to discussions that involve the lives and experiences of BGLQT people (Lipkin, 1995).

Kevin Jennings, a former high school teacher and former director of GLSEN, has written a helpful resource for history teachers: *Becoming visible: Reader in gay and lesbian history for high school and college students* (1994). There are also other curricular resources available that can support teachers to expand their discussion of the Holocaust and include information about how gay men and lesbians, Roma, disabled people, and other groups were also targeted for extermination in Nazi concentration camps (http://www.kean.edu/~hrc/curriculum.htm#high). Additionally there are helpful videos and lesson plans available that talk about Bayard Rustin, a key leader in the civil rights movement who was silenced because he was gay. GLSEN has produced a useful teacher's guide to accompany a PBS film that helps present some of these stories that are often omitted from traditional texts. The film is called *Out of the Past: The Struggle for Gay and Lesbian Rights in America*, and the free guide is available online (http://www.glsen.org/cgi-bin/iowa/all/booklink/record/1507.html). The gay liberation movement that emerged in the late 1960s due to many of the post-WWII social issues that gave rise to the civil rights movement is depicted in the film, *Before Stonewall* (Scagliotti, Schiller, & Rosenberg, 1984). This film can add to any unit that discusses the social, economic, and political events that led up to the civil rights movement. Finally, any discussion of current events or local issues related to same-sex marriage, gay and lesbian adoption, gay–straight alliances, and other school events can provide rich opportunities for lessons on local and national political processes, respectful debate, critical thinking, and student engagement.

Social Studies curricula are valuable sites where the political, intellectual, social, economic, and religious impacts of peoples' identities and experiences can be explored. When seeking out ways to include BGLQT history and social movements in class discussions, it is important to always attend to the intersectionality of issues and identities; that is recognizing how race, ethnicity, class background, gender, and sexual orientation intersect and overlap in ways that impact how people from marginalized groups have been treated by people in power. An extensive list of lesson plans on issues related to current events, law, history, and social issues are available online at http://www.safeschoolscoalition.org/RG-lessonplans.html.

4.4.3 Biology

Introducing critical thinking in the science classroom may seem somewhat challenging for teachers who have been presented with the concept that the sciences are objective and offer clear right and wrong answers to questions about the nature of things. However, there is much interesting work about introducing critical inquiry into the science classroom and encouraging students to question how scientific knowledge is created, validated, and accepted as true (Fifield & Swain, 2002; Herbes-Sommers, 2003; Kumashiro, 2004; Lehr, 2007). Art Lipkin and others have written about curriculum projects that explore the concept of homosexuality and examine it from biological, sociological, and historical perspectives (Lehr, 2007; Lipkin, 1995). This can contribute to the ongoing conversation of "nature versus nurture" and how laboratory-based scientific research can answer certain questions, but may leave other questions unanswerable.

Another topic that can be introduced in science classrooms is the question of gender identity and expression and the male–female binary. Kevin Kumashiro (2004) offers an example of such a lesson using the case of intersex children to question dominant conceptions of sex and gender (pp. 87–94). His proposed lesson includes information related to reproduction, chromosomal and hormonal influences on embryonic development, as well as how biological sex informs and is related to social norms related to gender. Related to this topic is the discussion of "sex hormones" in Biology textbooks and the representation of testosterone as the male hormone and estrogen as the female hormone. Nehm and Young (2008) conducted an analysis of eight widely used American high school biology text books and found that every one presented these steroid hormones as sex-specific, a notion that was disproved in scientific and medical literature in the 1930s. Nehm & Young present compelling evidence for biology teachers to use this oversimplification and misrepresentation of scientific data in text books as way to explore how culture and science influence each other. This is an example of how science education can be one way of "reinforcing, perpetuating, or justifying socio-cultural world views" (p. 1186). These authors clearly argue that "the scientific data on steroid hormones fly in the face of these socio-cultural standpoints: they neither suggest a clear-cut biochemical definition of male and female nor support a conceptual separation between sexual and non-sexual biochemical physiology" (p. 1187). As a result, science educators are urged to move away from terms such as "sex hormones" that are widely used in texts and use more accurate terms such as "steroid hormones" and to use this topic as a departure point for critical examinations of science and how it influences our constructions of sex and gender.

A third area to keep in mind is when lessons lead to unintended discussions of gender and sexuality, such as discussions of "homozygous" or "heterozygous" terms in genetics. By ignoring the laughs and the side comments that often erupt during discussions of these terms, teachers send messages to their students that they either are uncomfortable addressing issues or that being homosexual is something shameful that is not to be discussed. Rather, by addressing these jokes with a discussion about Greek and Latin root words as well as how science creates terms for new concepts educators can capitalize on a teachable moment, this discussion about language and science can help explore how the historical medicalization of certain terms, such as "homosexual" can create and perpetuate harmful stereotypes that sexual diversity is a disease or mental defect. Related to information taught in science courses is health and sexual education curricula.

4.4.4 Health and Sexual Education

Health and sexual education curricula have been a constant source of controversy: How much information should be taught in schools? At what age should such courses begin? Do schools have a responsibility to teach about public health issues related to safer sex practices and contraception or should that remain the responsibility of parents? How successful is abstinence-only education? The contexts and constraints on sexuality education differ greatly depending on the standards of each state or province as well as differences due to urban and rural divides. In a recent study of rural educators, some of the reported reasons for this variation between urban and rural schools is attributed to several causes: greater religiosity in rural communities; greater scrutiny of administrators' decisions by the church, school board, and community; and greater physical proximity and emotional closeness between rural educators and their students (Blinn-Pike, 2008). These differences are important for educators to be aware of as they enter a new community or school.

Although it is beyond the scope of this book to examine these variations in depth, it is important to note the impacts of abstinence-only-until-marriage programs in some parts of the United States since 1996. President Bill Clinton signed the Personal Responsibility and Work Opportunity Reconciliation Act which laid the foundation for these programs. In 2004, President George W. Bush promised to double federal funding for abstinence programs (Fisher, 2009). In recent years, the tide seems to be turning: in 2008, 17 U.S. states either refused to accept federal funds tied to abstinence-only programs or have passed laws requiring comprehensive sex education (Ashcraft, 2008). In May 2009, President Obama proposed cutting federal funding for abstinence-only programs in favor of a more comprehensive approach to sexual education (Jayson, 2009). We know that providing students a forum in which to learn about and discuss issues related to sexual and reproductive health is essential to their academic persistence and success (Ashcraft, 2008; Walters & Hayes, 2007). Research also demonstrates that BGLQT students who attend schools where abstinence-only sexual education curriculum is in place report higher levels of victimization related to their sexual orientation and gender identity than other students, and less comfort talking one-on-one with school personnel about BGLQT issues (Fisher, 2009; Kosciw et al., 2008, p. 136).

Health and sexual education classes used to be the only place where any mention of sexual identity, orientation, or behavior was discussed in schools and this was usually in relation to HIV and AIDS prevention programs (Lipkin, 1995). This one-sided presentation of issues related to BGLQT people tended to present a negative perspective of BGLQT sexual behaviors and life experiences. Richard Friend referred to this as *systematic inclusion,* or the repeated or regular inclusion of information about BGLQT people in a negative light (Friend, 1993). This systematic inclusion combined with the *systematic exclusion* of positive and well-rounded perspectives about BGLT people and their lives perpetuates harmful myths that all BGLQT people are promiscuous and are at risk for HIV, AIDS, and other sexually transmitted infections. More recently, Michelle Fine has called this an "active silence" (Fine, 2005). One gay youth articulated how this active silence impacted him by explaining, "if you aren't represented when they talk about *human sexuality* – you're not human. You can't be, because you're not included. You're not included. And that's fucked up" (cited in Fisher, 2009, p. 71).

Arthur Lipkin also warns about the possibility of "medicalization" of homosexuality and that this approach can teach the belief that BGLQT people are deviant and sick (Lipkin, 1999, p. 343). This warning is an important one as this is often the only time same-sex behaviors are discussed in schools. For example, AIDS and HIV are presented in one widely used abstinence-only text, *Sex Respect,* as follows:

> AIDS (Acquired Immune Deficiency Syndrome), the STD most common among homosexuals, bisexuals, and IV drug users, has now made its way into heterosexual circles...There is another form of sexual activity that causes an especially high risk of HIV infection. In such activity body openings are used in ways for which they were not designed...[W]hile AIDS is fatal and has no cure, the behaviour that leads to AIDS can be prevented through high personal standards and strong character (as cited in Kempner & Batchelder, 2004, pp. 10–11).

This factually incorrect statement perpetuates harmful stereotypes about BGLQT people and implies that people who engage in behaviors that are extramarital, non-heterosexual, non-monogamous, and non-procreative, lack "high personal standards and strong character." These messages combined with the active silencing around gender and sexual diversity are harmful to all youth.

In one study, researchers reported the ongoing homophobic jokes and remarks that went unchallenged during one teacher's lesson on AIDS and HIV. The lesson began with the teacher first asking if the students knew what AIDS stood for and a student replied, "homo." The teacher ignored this remark and answered the question herself. She then asked about HIV and got the same answer: "homo," which she ignored again. This then allowed the rest of the lesson to be peppered with homophobic comments and insults. Additionally, she implicitly perpetuated misinformation that only gay people are at risk for HIV or AIDS (Fields & Hirschman, 2007). Although it is important to inform students about the risks involved in unprotected sex, it is dangerous to imply that heterosexual behaviors may not be as risky as homosexual behaviors.

Fields and Hirschman use this example to point out that sexuality is not merely a private issue, rather it is deeply imbedded throughout public life. They explain that, "sexual desires, behaviors, and norms inform identity claims, media representations, and educational policies. Sexuality is an experience and institution at work in interactions among citizens in the workplace, courts, schools, streets, and homes" (p. 20). They advocate for a citizenship approach to sexuality education that can "recognize (or fail to recognize) one another as fully enfranchised members of a society" (p. 5) and can provide validation and inclusion in community life for diverse identities, families, and relationships.

In order to combat such misconceptions, health and sexual education courses should offer information not only on sexual behaviors, but also on relationship issues and on healthy decision making. One example of this is Seattle's Family Life and Sexual Health (FLASH) curriculum which introduces the concept of the Kinsey scale, the differences between sexual identities and behaviors, as well as the historical and social contexts of anti-gay prejudice and discrimination (Lipkin, 1999, p. 344). Another valuable conceptual model to introduce is Gayle Rubin's concept of the "charmed circle" and the "outer limits" of sexualities in our culture (Rubin, 1984/1993). In this model she presents two concentric circles that represent cultural values regarding various sexualities. In the inner, "charmed" circle, which includes the "good, normal, natural, and blessed sexuality," she includes heterosexual, married, monogamous, procreative, non-commercial, in pairs, in a relationship, same generation, in private, no pornography, bodies only, and "vanilla." In the "outer limits" which represent "bad, abnormal, unnatural, damned sexualities" she lists homosexual, unmarried, promiscuous, non-procreative, commercial, alone or in groups, casual, cross-generational, in public, pornography, with manufactured objects, and sadomasochistic (p. 13). Although the original text is more appropriate for university students, the framework can be easily adapted to a high school class discussion to help students think about how various forms of sexuality are valued or reviled in public life. Educators can use this model to help students understand why certain behaviors and scientific facts are deemed appropriate for inclusion in text books and formal curricula and others are censored.

Finally, it is important to recognize that many educators called on to teach sexual health do not feel adequately prepared to address such diverse and complex issues (Westwood & Mullan, 2007). Often these courses are assigned to the Physical Education or Health teachers, but this topic should not be seen as exclusively their domain. For example, in one Colorado school the Biology and Social Science teachers came together to design a course that would meet the needs and interests of their students (Michner, 2006). In the Canadian Province of Quebec, the five hours a year of sexual education classes were removed from the curriculum and teachers in all subject areas are now expected to integrate topics related to sexual education throughout their courses (Gouvernement du Quebec, 2004). Although this has raised some concern among educators, the philosophy behind the change is to integrate lessons related to sexuality throughout the curriculum so that all members of the school community are responsible for ensuring that students learn about sexuality issues in the context of other content areas.

4.4.5 Mathematics

It may seem difficult to conceptualize how to integrate issues related to gender and sexual diversity in math courses, but it can be done. For example, when creating basic word problems and the gender and the relationships of people in word problems, teachers should be mindful of the names they choose and the situations they set up. If they use scenarios where "Bobby buys Suzie a dozen roses for $x..." then they should also incorporate word problems where Bobby buys Chris or John a box of chocolates so as to offer a balanced set of experiences. Students might react strongly the first few times they hear these types of examples, but once they learn that it is a regular occurrence, they will stop reacting to the novelty of it and you will have provided inclusion and visibility to students where they previously had none.

A second approach can be to incorporate information about BGLQT people when studying charts, graphs, or statistics. There are some really interesting and relevant statistics available about the experiences of BGLQT youth in schools and the prevalence of bullying and harassment, available through GLSEN (www.glsen.org), the California Safe Schools Coalition (http://www.casafeschools.org/), and the Gender Public Advocacy Coalition (www.gpac.org). These teaching tools can provide students current and relevant statistics as well as helping them learn important social issues and math literacy skills.

A third approach builds on earlier discussions of learning to think more critically in general about information that is presented to us using numbers, statistics, and charts and graphs. Helping students learn about how statistics can be used to present different sides of an argument and to tell a certain story is also an important math lesson. Kevin Kumashiro writes at length about this and offers several valuable suggestions from his own classroom experiences in his book, *Against common sense: Teaching and learning toward social justice* (Kumashiro, 2004).

4.4.6 Fine and Performing Arts

Perrotti and Westheimer point out in the title of their book, *When the drama club is not enough: Lessons from the safe schools program for gay and lesbian students* (2001), that the Fine and Performing Arts departments are often the places in schools where BGLQT youth feel included and supported. Although these curricular areas don't often explicitly integrate issues related to gender and sexual orientation, the climate of creativity, performance, and exploring others' identities, emotions, and experiences may allow students to feel more comfortable with themselves if they don't fit in to the mainstream culture of their school community. However, in addition to continuing to foster these creative and supportive environments, teachers in these courses can also engage students in projects that do explicitly explore issues related to gender and sexual diversity.

As mentioned earlier, the use of theatre to explore the experiences of others and learn about new identities can be extremely productive (Callaghan, 2007). Drama and Speech teachers can select monologues, scenes, and plays that allow students to explore different gender roles and expressions, relationship configurations, and events. High school productions of *The Laramie Project*, and other plays that explicitly address issues of gender and sexual diversity offer students the opportunity to learn about and experience the impacts of homophobia and heterosexism through the play (Kaufman, Fondakowski, & Tectonic Theatre Project, 2001).

In addition to the performing arts, the visual arts can be another space where students' diverse identities and expressions can be encouraged to emerge. In addition to traditional art projects, students can be asked to reflect on various themes such as family, love, identity, home and then produce collages, quilts, photo essays, and paintings that express their understandings of these themes (Wells, 2007). The use of photography as a way to engage students in difficult concepts can be extremely productive as scholars who use "photo-voice" have reported (Rose, 2002). Photo-voice projects start with a common theme or question and ask participants to go and shoot images with that question in mind. Once the images have been captured (disposable cameras work well if your school doesn't have access to photography equipment), then the students talk about why they took certain photos and what they represent (Pink, 2000). Then you may have them choose one or two images that they prefer and then compose a caption for them. These final images can be hung as a "show" for the school community to generate further discussion around the chosen question or theme.

In addition to these common curricular areas, there is also much room for inclusion and exploration in elective courses such as psychology, sociology, anthropology, and art history. One such elective has been recently introduced in the British Columbia curriculum. Social Justice 12 is an upper-level course that encourages students to explore various "isms" and how they are interconnected and impact people's lives. For example, in the curriculum guide for the course one of the proposed outcomes for students in the course is to

> identify and define a range of concepts and terms of social justice (e.g., ableism, ageism, anthropocentrism, colonialism, consumerism, cultural imperialism, dignity, discrimination, diversity, economic imperialism, economic liberalization, empowerment, equality, equity, ethics, extremism, fairness, feminism, fundamentalism, genocide, globalization, hate crime, hegemony, heterosexism, homophobia, human rights, humanitarianism, humility, inclusion, individual responsibility, marginalization, misogyny, oppression, peace, persecution, power, prejudice, privilege, racism, sexism, speciesism, stereotype, stewardship, systemic, transformational leadership, truth, value, worth) (Province of British Columbia, 2008, p. 34)

This long list of terms related to social justice indicates that many teachers in British Columbia are interested in teaching students about how layers of social difference intersect and impact people's lives. This curriculum also explores ethics, belief systems, students' own biases, and prejudices as well as how to exercise and express critical judgment. This elective course is a wonderful example of how issues related to gender and sexual diversity can be integrated in productive and meaningful ways into the secondary school curriculum.

4.5 Extracurricular Activities

In addition to incorporating information and activities that address gender and sexual diversity in classroom curricula, there are also many opportunities to create safer and more inclusive spaces through extracurricular or co-curricular activities. Although there are many possibilities of ways to embrace and include gender and sexual diversity in non-class-related activities, the three that I will address here are gay–straight alliances, school-wide initiatives, and arts and athletics activities.

4.5.1 Gay–Straight Alliances

Student-led Gay–Straight Alliances (GSAs) have been growing in number and impact since the first documented group started in Concord, Massachusetts in 1989 (Macgillivray, 2007). There are now over 3,000 GSAs registered in the United States with the Gay, Lesbian, and Straight Education Network. As encouraging as this number sounds, a recent research report published by GLSEN showed that less than a quarter (22%) of U.S. students surveyed report having a GSA in their school (GLSEN, 2007). In Canada, there are fewer documented GSAs and there is currently no national organization that explicitly aims to coordinate and support such student groups. EGALE Canada has put new resources into such a project and is currently developing a website to provide resources and information to youth and educators starting and continuing such groups in their schools.

   As GSAs have grown in number and spread across the United States, they have been the source of legal controversies. Many school boards have tried to prevent these clubs from meeting on school grounds in spite of legislation that requires them to do so if other extracurricular clubs are given that access (GLSEN, 2002; Macgillivray, 2007; Meyer & Stader, 2009). The work of several of these student groups affirmed important protections for GSAs. Through court challenges around the country, judges supported the GSAs and mandated school boards to allow them to meet on school grounds based on the 1984 Federal Equal Access Act (*Boyd County High School Gay Straight Alliance v. Board of Education of Boyd County, Ky.*, 2003; *East High GSA v. Salt Lake City Board of Education*, 1999; *Straights and Gays for Equity v. Osseo Area Schools*, 2006). In spite of these clear and repeated legal decisions, students and their supporters continue to face opposition in trying to establish GSAs in their home communities (Gurney, 2007; Ochalla, 2007). There have been no similar legal challenges in Canada; however, there have been news reports of informal resistance by administrators to student efforts to create such a group at their school.

In recent years there has also been a growing body of research that has investigated the impacts of GSAs on school climate (Fischer & Kosciw, 2006; Szlacha, 2003) as well as the experiences of students who have been involved in such organizations (Goodenow, Szalacha, & Westhimer, 2006; Macgillivray, 2005; Mayo, 2004a; Sampson, 2000). These studies indicate that schools that have GSAs are more welcoming of all kinds of diversity, including racial, ethnic, and religious as well as gender and sexual diversity. These schools are places where gay, lesbian, bisexual, and transgender students and family members feel safer and experience a greater sense of belonging. For teachers and other youth workers who are interested in supporting students to start a gay–straight alliance or other diversity support and advocacy group, there are some helpful books and online resources available to support these efforts (GLSEN, 2007; Macgillivray, 2007; Wells, 2006).

In addition to establishing a student group that meets regularly to address issues related to gender and sexual diversity there are other school-wide initiatives that have been created to increase awareness and inspire school change and improve attitudes toward gay, lesbian, bisexual, questioning, and transgender people.

4.5.2 School-Wide Initiatives

School-wide initiatives are projects that may be initiated by faculty or students but generally include either a full day or a full week of activities. A few of the more widespread activities include The Day of Silence, No Name Calling Week, Wear Pink Day, and Allies day. The "Day of Silence" is a somewhat controversial event that began in 1996 at the University of Virginia when a group of students chose to remain silent for one day to call attention to the anti-BGLQT name-calling and harassment at their school. In 2007, over 5,000 middle and high schools in the United States and Canada participated. There has been backlash in some communities against this event, but students and teachers who have participated attest that it is generally a non-confrontational, yet empowering way to highlight issues of silencing and invisibility faced by BGLQT people and families in a school community. Their website (www.dayofsilence.org) provides guidance and free resources to help student groups organize this event in their school community.

"No Name Calling Week" was inspired by James Howe's novel *The Misfits*, which is a story of a group of friends who decide to try to combat the bullying they've experienced in school. This event happens annually and has grown into a nationwide phenomenon since it was first organized in March of 2004. There are free downloadable resources on the website (www.nonamecallingweek.org), as well as a kit that can be purchased online. This event is targeted toward students in Grades 5–8 and explicitly addresses biased forms of name-calling and harassment that happens between students, including homophobia and transphobia. Many school-wide organizing ideas as well as classroom activities, such as poster contests and readers' theatre presentations, are available.

"Wear pink day" is an event that has gathered much support in Canada due to its beginnings in a high school in Nova Scotia (Mills, 2007; Staff, 2008). Early in the school year, a Grade 9 student was targeted for homophobic bullying when he wore a pink shirt to school. To show their solidarity and reduce the bullying, two male Grade 12 students, Travis Price and DJ Shepherd bought over 25 pink shirts to distribute at school the next day. Although this event has gotten much support in schools across Canada, in many regions, it has been turned into a generic campaign against bullying and little discussion has been included about the homophobic nature of the initial incident. For example, Nova Scotia's government has declared the second Thursday of every school year as "Stand up against bullying day," and students are encouraged to wear pink to spread the "anti-bullying message" (Mills, 2007).

"Ally week" is an event organized by the Gay, Lesbian, and Straight Education Network and is held every October to end anti-BGLQT bullying and harassment in K–12 schools by building ties with allies. Allies are identified as people who advocate for the equality of a marginalized group, but do not identify as a member of that group. In the case of this event, most allies identify as heterosexual or normatively gendered or cisgendered. The goal of this event is to get students to sign an ally pledge to intervene in incidents of anti-BGLQT bullying and harassment. This event is a positive way to reach out to supportive students and get them involved in efforts to promote a safer and more inclusive school environment. By passing out stickers or providing other positive recognition for those who sign the pledge, you can build a strong visual presence of students who wish to have a school that is more positive and inclusive of bisexual, gay, lesbian, queer questioning, and transgender individuals and families. In addition to these school-wide initiatives, there are additional co-curricular opportunities for education and inclusion around gender and sexual diversity concerns.

4.5.3 Student Government, Arts and Athletics

Getting student leaders involved in efforts to improve school cultures is an important element of successful, long-term initiatives. Student leaders are often involved in multiple aspects of the school community including student council, athletics teams, as well as arts programs. In order to offer these students multiple opportunities to learn about gender and sexual diversity and provide leadership to the school community in these areas, it is important to use these activities as opportunities for deeper learning and engagement. Gay–Straight Alliances were mentioned earlier as a specific student group that may work regularly on these issues; however there are other groups that need to be implicated as well.

Student council and other student leadership activities are an important place to start. As these are often elected members that have the support of their peers, their actions and decisions can help set an important standard in a class or a school. Providing after-school or weekend leadership workshops and retreats that address issues of diversity and difference can help these students provide positive role modeling in behavior and attitudes. Such events should work to address multiple levels of diversity including race, ethnicity, gender, language, religion, as well as gender and sexual diversity.

Sports teams can also hold a high degree of social power in a school community. If coaches consciously work to address incidents of sexism and homophobia with their players and role model positive behaviors and correct harmful ones, the players will learn to act differently. One valuable resource available to help coaches work with their teams is "It Takes a team." This kit was developed by Pat Griffin at the University of Massachusetts, Amherst and is available online at www.ittakesateam.org. This kit specifically addresses how gender and sexual orientation stereotypes can harm athletes, coaches, and the team environment. The kit includes a video, action guides, posters, stickers, and additional resources that can be helpful for coaches and athletes at the secondary and university level.

In addition to members of sports teams, students involved in the visual and performing arts can use their interests and talent to present creative and artistic ways to promote support for gender and sexual diversity in schools. Although this can be incorporated into the curriculum as mentioned earlier, for many schools arts-based activities may only happen after the school day is over. Using drama and theatrical spaces is one way to help students explore the affective elements involved in unlearning past prejudice and negative stereotypes. In Tonya Callaghan's chapter on using the Theatre of the Oppressed, she presents five different scripts that she has used with high school students to help them explore issues related to homophobia and religious beliefs (Callaghan, 2007). There are also traveling theater troupes that present well-crafted, age-appropriate plays that engage the audience in the story. Building on the strength of theatre arts to help transform school cultures allows students and educators to address the personal and emotional issues that are usually ignored in the standard curriculum. A second avenue for exploration of these issues in the arts is using visual arts to explore student identities' and experiences. Kris Wells has written about the productive use of such artistic devices as photo-voice, poetry, collage, and quilting to create visual displays of queer youth experiences (Wells, 2007). Providing students multi-media in which to explore their identities and communicate their experiences to others is another way to involve students and empower them to participate in transforming their schools' formal and informal curricula.

4.6 Conclusion

The practical applications suggested in this chapter align with the curriculum theories presented in Chapter 1 and are meant to offer new and experienced educators a starting point for developing their own resources, lessons, and projects that will help create safer and more inclusive learning environments. Although some school environments may make it more difficult to openly begin integrating these topics into the curriculum, there are many schools that are ready and in need of such instruction. A study in Ontario reports that the fear of parental backlash is the most prevalent obstacle for why educators don't respond to BGLQT issues in school. Although these fears were not corroborated with any known stories of backlash, this unspoken threat causes caring teachers to censor themselves and prevents them from taking perceived risks in their classroom (Schneider & Dimito, 2008). The authors in this study do acknowledge that individual teachers need to carefully examine their own school communities before choosing to teach about potentially controversial issues. Some of the items they recommend considering include (a) levels of support from various sources, (b) attitudes of people such as colleagues, administrators, students, and parents, (c) the nature of the activity involving BGLQT issues, and (d) available resources (p. 68). The last chapter of this book also presents a model for reading and understanding a school's culture in order to help educators make strategic and informed decisions about how to take action and cultivate support for inclusion of gender and sexual diversity topics in the curriculum.

Through being more conscious of daily approaches to teaching and classroom management, the implicit and explicit lessons teachers present through the texts they choose, units they develop, and assessments they create, teachers can have a significant impact on improving the overall experience of students' lives. Although there are many aspects of school that shape students' experiences, the formal curriculum is an important one. This chapter was written to help show how to integrate the theories and concepts presented in the first part of this book into one's classroom practice at any grade level. If you do create a new lesson or project that applies some of the concepts and principles introduced in this text, please share them with your colleagues, post them to a local educators' wiki, your own Web site, or e-mail them to me at Elizabeth.meyer@mail.mcgill.ca and I'll be happy to share them with the educational community. It is only through building community and mutually supporting each others' efforts that educators can help improve the experiences of their students.

References

Apple, M. (2000). *Official knowledge: Democratic education in a conservative age* (2nd ed.). New York: Routledge.

Ashcraft, C. (2008). So much more than "sex ed": Teen sexuality as a vehicle for improving academic success and democratic education for diverse youth. *American Educational Research Journal, 45*(3), 631–667.

Bickmore, K. (1999). Why discuss sexuality in elementary school? In W. J. Letts & J. T. Sears (Eds.), *Queering elementary education: Advancing the dialogue about sexualities in schooling* (pp. 14–25). Lanham, MD: Rowman Littlefield.

Blackburn, M. V. (2002). Disrupting the (Hetero)normative: Exploring literacy performances and identity work with queer youth. *Journal of Adolescent & Adult literacy, 46*(4), 312–324.

Blackburn, M. V., & Buckley, J. F. (2005). Teaching queer-inclusive English language arts. *Journal of Adolescent & Adult Literacy, 49*(3), 202–212.

Blaise, M. (2005). *Playing it straight!: Uncovering gender discourses in the early childhood classroom*. New York: Routledge Press.

Blinn-Pike, L. (2008). Sex education in rural schools in the United States: Impact of rural educators' community identities. *Sex Education: Sexuality, Society and Learning, 8*(1), 77–92.

Bouley, T. (2007). The silenced family: Policies and perspectives on the inclusion of children's literature depicting gay/lesbian families in public elementary classrooms. In I. Killoran &

K. P. Jimenez (Eds.), *"Unleashing the unpopular": Talking about sexual orientation and gender diversity in education* (pp. 140–147). Olney, MD: Association for Childhood Education International.

Boyd County High School Gay Straight Alliance v. Board of Education of Boyd County, Ky. (258 F. Supp. 2d 667 (E. D. KY) 2003).

Callaghan, T. (2007). Acting out: Using Agusto Boal's theatre of the oppressed techniques to teach about homophobic incidents in catholic schools. In I. Killoran & K. P. Jimenez (Eds.), *"Unleashing the unpopular": Talking about sexual orientation and gender diversity in education* (pp. 129–139). Olney, MD: Association for Childhood Education International.

Chamberlain v. Surrey School District No. 36 (4 SCR 710 2002).

Chasnoff, D. (Writer) (1996). It's Elementary: Talking about gay issues in school. In H. S. Cohen & D. Chasnoff (Producer). San Francisco, CA: Ground Spark.

COLAGE. (2009). Facts. Retrieved January 25, 2009, from http://www.colage.org/resources/facts.htm

De Haan, L., & Nijland, S. (2000). *King & King*. Berkeley, CA: Ten Speed Press.

DePalma, R., & Atkinson, E. (Eds.). (2008). *Invisible boundaries: Addressing sexualities equality in children's worlds*. Stoke on Trent, UK: Trentham Books.

DeVries, R., Zan, B., Hildebrandt, C., Edmiaston, R., & Sales, C. (Eds.). (2001). *Developing constructivist early childhood curriculum: Practical principles and activities*. New York: Teachers College Press.

East High Gay/Straight Alliance v. Board of Education of Salt Lake City School District (81 F. Supp. 2d 1166, 1197 (D. Utah 1999) 1999).

Fields, J., & Hirschman, C. (2007). Citizenship lessons in abstinence-only sexuality education. *American Journal of Sexuality Education, 2*(2), 3–25.

Fierstein, H. (2002). *The sissy duckling*. New York: Simon & Schuster.

Fifield, S., & Swain, H. L. (2002). Heteronormativity and Common Sense in Science (Teacher) Education. In R. Kissen (Ed.), *Getting ready for Benjamin: Preparing teachers for sexual diversity in the classroom* (pp. 177–189). Lanham, MD: Rowman Littlefield.

Fine, M. (2005). Desire: The morning (and 15 years) after. *Feminism & Psychology, 15*(1), 54–60.

Fischer, S. N., & Kosciw, J. (2006, April 7–11). *The importance of gay-straight alliances: Associations with teacher and staff response to homophobia*. Paper presented at the American Educational Research Association, San Francisco, CA.

Fisher, C. M. (2009). Queer youth experiences with abstinence-only-until-marriage sexuality education: "I can't get married so where does that leave me?" *Journal of LGBT Youth, 6*(1), 61–79.

Friend, R. (1993). Choices, not closets: Heterosexism and homophobia in schools. In L. Weis & M. Fine (Eds.), *Beyond silenced voices: Class, race, and gender in United States schools* (pp. 209–235). Albany, NY: State University of New York Press.

GLSEN. (2002). *Laws and policies affecting GLBT youth*. New York: The Gay, Lesbian, and Straight Education Network.

GLSEN. (2007). *Gay-straight alliances: Creating safer schools for LGBT students and their allies* (No. GLSEN Research Brief). New York: Gay, Lesbian and Straight Education Network.

Goodenow, C., Szalacha, L., & Westhimer, K. (2006). School support groups, other school factors, and the safety of sexual minority adolescents. *Psychology in the Schools, 43*(5), 573–589.

Gouvernement du Quebec. (2004). *Quebec education program, secondary education*. Retrieved July 24, 2009, from http://www.mels.gouv.qc.ca/DGFJ/dp/programme_de_formation/secondaire/qepsecfirstcycle.htm

Griffin, P., Lee, C., Waugh, G., & Beyer, C. (2004). Describing roles that gay-straight alliances play in schools: From individual support to school change. *Journal of Gay & Lesbian Issues in Education, 1*(3), 7–22.

Gurney, K. (2007, October 25–31). Controversy over school club divides the Farmington community *Alibi.com*

Harper v. Poway Unified School District (445 F.3d 1166 (9th Cir.) 2006).

Herbes-Sommers, C. (Writer) (2003). Race – The power of an illusion: Episode 1-"The difference between us" [film]. In S. Haller (Producer). San Francisco, CA: USA: California Newsreel.

Jayson, S. (2009). Obama budget cuts funds for abstinence-only sex education [Electronic Version]. *USA Today*. Retrieved July 24, 2009, from http://www.usatoday.com/news/health/ 2009-05-11-abstinence-only_N.htm

Jennings, K. (1994). *Becoming visible: Reader in gay and lesbian history for high school and college students*. Boston: Alyson Publications.

Kaufman, M., Fondakowski, L., & Tectonic Theatre Project. (2001). *The Laramie project*. New York: Dramatists Play Service Inc.

Kempner, M. E., & Batchelder, M. (2004). *Keeping our youth "Scared chaste" SIECUS curriculum review: Sex Respect, A fear-based abstinence-only-until-marriage curriculum, junior high and senior high school students*. New York: SIECUS.

Killoran, I., & Jimenez, K. P. (Eds.). (2007). *"Unleashing the unpopular": Talking about sexual orientation and gender diversity in education*. Olney, MD: Association for Childhood Education International.

Kosciw, J., Diaz, E., & Gretytak, E. (2008). *2007 National School Climate Survey: The experiences of lesbian, gay, bisexual, and transgender youth in our nation's schools*. New York: GLSEN.

Kumashiro, K. (2004). *Against common sense: Teaching and learning toward social justice*. New York: Routledge Falmer.

LaGravenese, R. (Writer) (2006). Freedom writers [film]. USA: Paramount Pictures.

Lehr, J. L. (2007). Beyond nature: Critically engaging science to queer straight teachers. In N. Rodriguez & W. F. Pinar (Eds.), *Queering straight teachers: Discourse and identity in education* (pp. 33–64). New York: Peter Lang.

Letts, W. J., & Sears, J. T. (Eds.). (1999). *Queering elementary education: Advancing the dialogue about sexualities in schooling*. Lanham, MD: Rowman Littlefield.

Lipkin, A. (1995). The case for a gay and lesbian curriculum. In G. Unks (Ed.), *The gay teen* (pp. 31–52). New York: Routledge.

Lipkin, A. (1999). *Understanding homosexuality, changing schools*. Boulder, CO: Westview Press.

Macgillivray, I. K. (2005). Shaping democratic identities and building citizenship skills through student activism: Mexico's first gay-straight alliance. *Journal of Educational Excellence and Equity, 38*, 320–330.

Macgillivray, I. K. (2007). *Gay-straight alliances: A handbook for students, educators, and parents*. Binghamton, NY: Harrington Park Press.

Mayo, C. (2004a). *Disputing the subject of sex: Sexuality and public school controversies*. Lanham, MD: Rowman & Littlefield.

Mayo, C. (2004b). Queering school communities: Ethical curiosity and Gay-straight alliances. *Journal of Gay & Lesbian Issues in Education, 1*(3), 23–36.

Meyer, E. J. (2006). Gendered harassment in North America: School-based interventions for reducing homophobia and heterosexism. In C. Mitchell & F. Leach (Eds.), *Combating gender violence in and around schools* (pp. 43–50). Stoke on Trent, UK: Trentham Books.

Meyer, E. J., & Stader, D. (2009). Queer youth and the culture wars: From the classroom to the courtroom in Australia, Canada, and the United States. *Journal of LGBT Youth, 6*(2), 135–154.

Michner, J. A. (2006). Sex education: A success in our social-studies class. *Clearing House: A Journal of Educational Strategies, Issues and Ideas, 79*(5), 210–214.

Mills, M. (2007). Nova Scotia teens speak about 'wear pink' protest [Electronic Version]. *Xtra*. Retrieved July 30, 2008, from http://www.xtra.ca/public/viewstory.aspx? AFF_TYPE=3&STORY_ID=3689&PUB_TEMPLATE_ID=1.

Nehm, R. H., & Young, R. (2008). "Sex hormones" in secondary school biology textbooks. *Science & Education, 17*(10), 1175–1190.

Newman, L. (2000). *Heather has two mommies* (2nd ed.). Boston: Alyson Publications.

Ochalla, B. (2007, September 23). School board allows gay-straight alliance. Retrieved December 18, from http://www.mysocalledgaylife.com/ca/index.php?option=com_content&task= view&id=4953&Itemid=67

Perrotti, J., & Westheimer, K. (2001). *When the drama club is not enough: Lessons from the safe schools program for gay and lesbian students.* Boston: Beacon Press.

Pharr, S. (1988). *Homophobia: A weapon of sexism.* Little Rock, AR: Womens Project.

Pink, S. (2000). *Doing visual ethnography.* London: Sage.

Province of British Columbia. (2008). *Social justice 12: Integrated resource package.* Retrieved March 20, 2009, from http://www.bced.gov.bc.ca/irp/social_justice12/sj12irp2008.pdf

Ressler, P. (2005). Challenging normative sexual and gender identity beliefs through Romeo and Juliet. *English Journal, 95*(1), 52.

Richardson, J., & Parnell, P. (2005). *And Tango makes three.* New York: Simon & Schuster.

Rose, G. (2002). *Visual methodologies.* Thousand Oaks, CA: Sage.

Rubin, G. (1984/1993). Thinking sex: Notes for a radical theory of the politics of sexuality. In H. Abelove, M. A. Barale & D. M. Halperin (Eds.), *The lesbian and gay studies reader* (pp. 3–44). New York: Routledge.

Russell, S. T., Kostroski, O., McGuire, J.K., Laub, C., & Manke, E. . (2006). *LGBT Issues in the curriculum promotes school safety.* San Francisco, CA: California Safe Schools Coalition.

Sampson, P. C. (2000). Will participation in a gay/straight alliance mitigate risk behavior in gay and lesbian youth? Unpublished manuscript. Salem, MA: Salem State College.

Scagliotti, J., Schiller, G., & Rosenberg, R. (Writer) (1984). Before stonewall: The making of a gay and lesbian community [film]. USA: Frameline.

Schneider, M. S., & Dimito, A. (2008). Educators' beliefs about raising lesbian, gay, bisexual, and transgender issues in the schools: The experience in Ontario, Canada. *Journal of LGBT Youth, 5*(4), 49–71.

Schrader, A. M., & Wells, K. (2007). *Challenging silence, challenging censorship.* Ottawa, ON: Canadian Teachers' Federation.

Skowronski, S. (2008, April 3). *First amendment rights and sexual orientation harassment in schools.* Paper presented at the Annual meeting of the MPSA Annual National Conference.

Sleeter, C., & Grant, C. (1994). *Making choices for multicultural education: Five approaches to race, class and gender.* Toronto, ON: Maxwell Macmillan Canada.

Staff. (2008). Wednesday is wear pink day [Electronic Version]. *BCTF School staff Alert, 2007–08.* Retrieved January 25, 2009 from http://bctf.ca/publications/SchoolStaffAlert.aspx?id=15128

Steffe, L. P., & Gale, J. E. (Eds.). (1995). *Constructivism in education.* New York: Taylor & Francis.

Straights and Gays for Equity v. Osseo Area Schools (Civ. No. 05-21000 (JNE/FLN), Mn 2006).

Szlacha, L. (2003). Safer sexual diversity climates: Lessons learned from an evaluation of Massachusetts safe schools program for gay and lesbian students. *American Journal of Education, 110*(1), 58–88.

Walters, A. S., & Hayes, D. M. (2007). Teaching about sexuality: balancing contradictory social messages with professional standards. *American Journal of Sexuality Education, 2*(2), 27–49.

Wells, K. (2006). *Gay-straight student alliance handbook*: Canadian Teachers' Federation.

Wells, K. (2007). Diverse threads in social fabrics: Autobiography and arts-informed educational initiatives for social justice. In I. Killoran & K. P. Jimenez (Eds.), *"Unleashing the unpopular": Talking about sexual orientation and gender diversity in education* (pp. 117–128). Olney, MD: Association for Childhood Education International.

Westwood, J., & Mullan, B. (2007). Knowledge and attitudes of secondary school Teachers regarding sexual health education in England. *Sex education: Sexuality, society and learning, 7*(2), 143–159.

Willhoite, M. (1990). *Daddy's roommate.* Boston: Alyson Publications.

Zolotow, C. (1972). *William's doll.* Mexico: HarperCollins.

Chapter 5
Law and Policy Issues

Myths and misconceptions about law and policy:
(1) There are federal legal protections in the United States and Canada against discrimination based on one's gender identity or expression and sexual orientation.
(2) In order for teachers, administrators, and schools to avoid legal liability, it is preferable to avoid talking about controversial issues.
(3) Education professionals are held to the same legal standards as any other professional in society.

5.1 Introduction

Queer (bisexual, lesbian, gay, transgender, or BGLQT) youth are challenging the heteronormative cultures in schools by disclosing their sexual orientation at a younger age and with unprecedented regularity (Cloud, 2005). As the prevailing values of these traditionally heteronormative institutions are questioned, schools have become important battlegrounds in the culture wars between conservatives and progressives as they struggle to reframe public policies and national conversations about education. Unfortunately, many of these youth and their schools have been caught in the crosshairs over this contentious subject. Many conservative politicians and religious leaders vocally oppose same-sex marriage, promote a heterosexual-based abstinence-only sex education curriculum, and challenge local school district efforts to promote diversity education and create safer school climates. In this climate, school administrators and teachers are expected to act as gender and sexuality police and enforce conformity to heterosexual gender norms for the students at their schools (Lugg, 2006). At the same time, many queer youth continue to face discrimination, rejection, and hostility from peers, teachers, and administrators. In the context of this chapter, when I use the term "queer youth" I include not only BGLQT-identified youth, but also youth who are questioning their sexual orientation or gender identity, children of BGLQT parents, and heterosexual youth who have been targeted with homophobic harassment in schools or identify as BGLQT allies. All of these groups have directly felt the harmful impacts of sexism, gender normativity, homophobia, and heteronormativity in schools and have been involved in the cultural battles that have led to the legal cases and policy initiatives addressed here.

5.2 Canada

The current progressive political climate in Canada was achieved through a long and slow process of legislative reform that culminated in the adoption of the *Canadian Charter of Rights and Freedoms*. This important document was entrenched into the Canadian constitution by the Constitution Act in 1982 (Watkinson, 1999, p. 22). As part of the supreme law of Canada, this document superseded all existing laws, and for the first time the rights of all persons to be treated equally was given constitutional status. Although public education is governed by provincial statutes, all publicly funded institutions must abide by the spirit and letter of the *Charter* (Watkinson, 1999). This new constitution guaranteed protections for many historically marginalized groups. Sexual orientation, however, was not initially included as a protected class for equality rights under Section 15 of the *Canadian Charter of Rights and Freedoms*. The original language of this section reads as follows:

> Every individual is equal before and under the law and has the right to the equal protection and equal benefit of the law without discrimination and, in particular, without discrimination based on race, national or ethnic origin, religion, sex, age or mental or physical disability. (*Canadian Charter of Rights and Freedoms* (s. 15), 1982)

Although the federal government wasn't willing to explicitly include the phrase, "sexual orientation" in the *Charter,* other provinces had already established human rights codes that included this term. In 1977, the Province of Quebec led the way in the equality movement for sexual minorities by adding "sexual orientation" to its *Charter of Human Rights and Freedoms*. Ontario followed suit 9 years later. These were the first legal protections that clearly included sexual orientation as a protected class (Hurley, 2005).

5.2.1 Egan v. Canada

Although equality rights supported by the *Charter* were enforced starting in 1985, sexual minorities were not recognized as a protected class until 13 years later, following a unanimous decision of the Supreme Court of Canada in the landmark case of *Egan v. Canada* (1995). Although this case was not about discrimination in schools, it addressed the issue of access to public services; specifically, the definition of 'spouse' in the federal Old Age Security Act (Lahey, 1999). The ruling provided that discrimination based on sexual orientation was prohibited by s. 15 of the *Charter,* and the justices observed: "Sexual orientation is a deeply personal characteristic that is either unchangeable or changeable only at unacceptable personal costs, and so falls within the ambit of s. 15 protection as being analogous to the enumerated grounds" (*Egan v. Canada,*1995, para. 5). Although the justices ruled that such discrimination in this case was "justifiable," this decision effectively placed the category of sexual orientation on the list of protected groups in the *Charter.*

This case established the precedent to include sexual orientation as a protected class, and had "sexual orientation" read into the *Charter*. Every Canadian was guaranteed equal protection from discrimination based on sexual orientation. Although some provinces were slow to add the term "sexual orientation" to their individual human rights codes, this protection was federally guaranteed as a result of this important ruling.

Since the Supreme Court's 1995 decision in *Egan v. Canada,* various cases have tested the interpretation and application of the equality rights extended in that case. In the first case in an educational institution after Egan was decided was *Vriend v. Alberta* (1998). In this case, Delwin Vriend, an employee of King's College, a Christian college in Edmonton, Alberta, was fired from his position as a lab coordinator, solely because of his homosexuality. King's College had instituted a position statement condemning homosexuality and requiring all students and employees to comply with the University's position. Vriend was called on to resign when he confirmed that he was homosexual, but he refused and was fired. He initially brought forward a human rights complaint; however, it was dismissed because the province of Alberta did not have sexual orientation listed as a protected class in its human rights legislation. In this case, the Supreme Court stated that not protecting individuals from discrimination based on sexual orientation was an "unjustified violation of s. 15 of the *Canadian Charter of Rights and Freedoms*," and ordered that the words "sexual orientation" be read into provincial human rights codes as a prohibited ground of discrimination (*Vriend v. Alberta,* 1998, p. 2).

5.2.2 Trinity Western University v. B.C. College of Teachers

The next test came in May 2001 when the Supreme Court of Canada heard a case from Trinity Western University (TWU), a private, religious institution that filed against the British Columbia College of Teachers (BCCT). In this instance, the BC professional teachers' organization had responded to a request from TWU to be fully responsible for its teacher training program, which it had previously shared with Simon Fraser University. Trinity Western University wanted more autonomy in the program in order to reflect its Christian worldview. The BCCT chose not to accredit this institution because it believed the institution was discriminating on the basis of sexual orientation in its demands on its students. TWU required its students to sign a statement that asserted they would "refrain from practices that are biblically condemned," including homosexuality (*Trinity Western University v. British Columbia College of Teachers,* 2001, para. 4).

In its decision, the British Columbia Supreme Court found in favor of TWU, stating that teachers could hold "sexist, racist, or homophobic beliefs" (para. 36). However, the Court also made the following distinction:

> Acting on those beliefs, however, is a very different matter. If a teacher in the public school system engages in discriminatory conduct, that teacher can be subject to disciplinary

proceedings. Discriminatory conduct by a public school teacher when on duty should always be subject to disciplinary proceedings [and] disciplinary measures can still be taken when discriminatory off-duty conduct poisons the school environment. (*Trinity Western v. British Columbia College of Teachers*, 2001, at para. 37)

Although this majority opinion sided with TWU and allowed them to continue mandating anti-gay beliefs in their future teachers, the judges made the important distinction between discriminatory behaviors and beliefs, which is common in cases regarding religious freedom. The decision clearly states that teachers may not discriminate overtly against their students but does not address the issue of the subtle and persistent homophobic behaviors that such attitudes can engender and the impact they have on a classroom or school community.

5.2.3 Kempling v. B.C. College of Teachers

The position that teachers may hold discriminatory beliefs as long as they do not act upon them in such a way as to create a "poisoned" school environment was reinforced in another BC case. In February 2004, a BC teacher, Chris Kempling, was suspended for one month for "conduct unbecoming" a teacher because he had published articles that were considered to be defaming of homosexuals in a local newspaper (*Kempling v. British Columbia College of Teachers*, 2004, para.1). The Christian teacher appealed this decision to the BC Supreme Court, but the court held that the BCCT was within its jurisdiction to suspend him. The court's rationale for its decision was based on the "wrongful public linking of his professional position to the off-duty expression of personally held discriminatory views in order to lend credibility to those views" (*Kempling v. British Columbia College of Teachers*, 2004, para. 2).

These cases have established a clear responsibility on the part of schools and their representatives to create learning environments that are free from discrimination. The final case discussed here demonstrates what happened when a school failed to provide such an environment.

5.2.4 School District 44 v. Jubran

Azmi Jubran, a student in Vancouver, was repeatedly called "gay," "faggot," and "homo" by his peers in secondary school. In addition to these verbal taunts, he was spit upon, shoved in class and the hallways, and even had his shirt burned. Jubran and his parents made repeated complaints to the school, and, after receiving no satisfactory response, they filed a human rights complaint in November 1996. In April 2002, the Human Rights Tribunal of British Columbia found that the school board in Vancouver had contravened the *Human Rights Code*, "by failing to provide a learning environment free of discriminatory harassment" (*School District No. 44 v. Jubran*, 2005, para. 2). This was an important decision because it affirmed the school's responsibility to protect students from discriminatory behavior, and to respond effectively and consistently to incidents of homophobic harassment. After a series of appeals, the fate of this case was decided on October 20, 2005, when the Supreme Court refused to hear a final appeal, and effectively upheld the lower court's decision. This was an important decision. The court acknowledged that the school had made some effort to discipline the students who had targeted Jubran individually, but said that it had not done enough. The court stated that the school needed to have communicated its code of conduct to students and provided teachers with resources and training on how to deal with homophobia (CLE Staff, 2005; Meyer, 2007). This case sent a clear message to educators that they must mobilize multiple resources and be proactive when addressing issues of school climate and student safety that relate directly to human rights protections.

As beneficial as the Jubran case was to clarifying the responsibilities of school boards to provide safe learning environments for students, there have been no legal cases in Canada that address the issues related to the rights of transgender youth in schools. However, there are documented cases of transgender youth transitioning in Canadian schools with the support of school personnel. In the Toronto District School Board they created a fully integrated team of professionals who worked closely with the student and her family to provide support and a clear line of communications during her transition. A few key strategies employed by the TDSB team that helped them be relatively successful in helping set the stage for this student's transition included (1) having a policy that supported the student's right to transition and the school had the responsibility to "grant him that right and to ensure his [sic] safety and comfort" (p. 41), (2) inviting a social worker with expertise in trans issues to work with the school's administration to identify potential barriers and solutions, (3) holding informational meetings to inform and educate the core instructional staff working with the student, (4) making contacts with local BGLQT community groups for resources and support, (5) holding meetings with the family, after briefing school staff, to discuss the transition plan, (6) informing the school's community police officer in order to help develop a plan that could best ensure the student's physical safety in and around school, and lastly (7) sending a letter out to all school staff announcing the date of the student's transition and providing basic information about her preferred name and pronouns. Other key advice offered by one of the youth workers from this experience: don't panic, build trust, inform youth of options, and connect trans youth and their families with community resources (p. 51). For a copy of the letter that was sent and a more detailed description of this case, please see Callender (2008).

As the above listed cases demonstrate, there are legal precedents that exist to protect students from discriminatory behavior in schools. However, many school boards and educators are ignorant of their legal responsibilities and fail to effectively implement policies, programs, and curricular materials that support full inclusion of sexual diversity in school communities.

5.3 United States of America

There are currently no federal protections that explicitly protect gay, lesbian, bisexual, and transgender people from discrimination in the United States. However, under various federal laws presented in this section, sexual minorities are implicitly entitled to the same protection as any other identifiable group. Due to this lack of explicit protection, there can be differing interpretations and applications of the law. In spite of this lack of explicit inclusion in federal protections, a variety of courts across the United States have begun holding school districts accountable for violating the rights of students who are being harassed or who have requested the right to form extracurricular groups that address their needs and interests. The main legal protections that have been applied in these cases include Equal Protection Clause of the Fourteenth Amendment, Title IX of the Education Acts, state non-discrimination laws, and The Equal Access Act.

5.3.1 Federal Protections and Case Studies

The Equal Protection Clause of the Fourteenth Amendment guarantees equal application of a law to all people in the United States (Macgillivray, 2007). An equal protection claim requires the student to show that school officials (1) did not fairly and consistently apply policies when dealing with the student, (2) were deliberately indifferent to the student's complaints, or (3) that the student was treated in a manner that was clearly unreasonable. The first example of this argument being successfully applied to a case of sexual orientation harassment in schools was in the case *Nabozny v. Podlesny* (1996) in Wisconsin. In this case, Jamie Nabozny was subjected to violent and persistent anti-gay harassment over several years in his school. As a result of this harassment, he had been hospitalized, dropped out of school, and attempted suicide (Lipkin, 1999). The federal appeals court for that region of the United States, the Seventh Circuit, decided in favor of the student. In their decision, the judges wrote that "...we are unable to garner any rational basis for permitting one student to assault another based on the victim's sexual orientation..." and the school district settled with Nabozny for $900,000 (Bochenek & Brown, 2001). More recently in a case in California, *Flores v. Morgan Hill* (2003), the court found sufficient evidence of deliberate indifference to the ongoing sexual orientation harassment of six students in this California School District, which resulted in a $1,100,000 settlement with the students (ACLU, 2004), and the requirement that the school district implement a training and education program for its administrators, faculty, and students (Dignan, 2004).

Title IX is another federal protection that exists to address issues of sexual orientation harassment in schools. It provides statutory protection for student-on-student sexual harassment under the following conditions (1) school personnel have actual knowledge of the harassment, (2) school officials demonstrate deliberate indifference or take actions that are clearly unreasonable, and (3) the harassment is so severe, pervasive, and objectively offensive that it can be said to deprive the victim(s) of access to the educational opportunities or benefits provided by the school (*Davis v. Monroe*, 1999). Several cases have successfully made the argument that Title IX protects students from peer sexual orientation harassment. For example, a California Federal District Court concluded that the Court finds no material difference between the instance in which a female student is subject to unwelcome sexual comments and advances due to her harasser's perception that she is a sex object, and the instance in which a male student is insulted and abused due to his harasser's perception that he is a homosexual, and therefore a subject of prey. In both instances, the conduct is a heinous response to the harasser's perception of the victim's sexuality, and is not distinguishable to this court. (*Ray v. Antioch Unified School District,* 2000)

In 2000, two important cases were decided that applied Title IX to incidences of homophobic harassment: *Ray v. Antioch Unified School District* (2000), and *Montgomery v. Independent School District* (2000). In both of these cases, separate federal district courts (California and Minnesota, respectively) decided that schools could be held liable under Title IX for acting with "deliberate indifference" toward students who have reported persistent and severe homophobic harassment at school. These decisions established important precedents for the cases that followed.

A few years later, a Kansas federal district court considered that the gender stereotyping and the related anti-gay harassment of a student who did not identify as gay was actionable under Title IX (*Theno v. Tonganoxie*, 2005). The court wrote that "the plaintiff was harassed because he failed to satisfy his peers' stereotyped expectations for his gender because the primary objective of plaintiff's harassers appears to have been to disparage his perceived lack of masculinity." Therefore, they concluded that the harassment of Dylan Theno was so "severe, pervasive, and objectively offensive that it effectively denied (him) an education in the Tonganoxie school district" (*Theno v. Tonganoxie*, 2005). The district settled with Dylan for a total of $440,000 (Trowbridge, 2005).

One case had a very different outcome. In *Doe v. Bellefonte School District* (2004), the U.S. Court of Appeals for the Third Circuit based in Pennsylvania, decided for the school district. It determined that campus administrators took Doe's complaints seriously, instituted a series of steps in response to complaints, and escalated punishment when necessary. Therefore, the district was not deliberately indifferent to the harassment of Doe.

The Equal Access Act (EAA) is another legal protection that is being used successfully to advance education around sexual diversity in schools through extracurricular diversity clubs. Peer support groups, commonly known as gay–straight alliances (GSAs), have become increasingly common in schools (Cloud, 2005; Fischer & Kosciw, 2006). Very little research is available on the efficacy of GSAs, but Fischer and Kosciw (2006) found that the presence of a GSA directly predicted greater school belonging, and indirectly predicted greater academic achievement for sexual-minority youth. Also Szlacha (2003) found in her evaluation of the Massachusetts Safe Schools Program that the presence of a GSA is the aspect "most strongly associated with positive sexual diversity climates" (73). This finding makes intuitive sense when considering the importance of supportive heterosexual peers to a positive experience for sexual-minority youth. However, GSAs are not always met with open-mindedness from students, teachers, administrators, parents, community members, and school boards. Since the late 1990s, there have been several cases of schools trying to exclude these groups from meeting on school grounds. Courts have consistently found that school districts have violated the EAA when banning GSA groups from meeting. *Straights and Gays for Equity v. Osseo Area Schools*(2006) and *White County High School Peers Rising in Diverse Education v. White County School District* (2006) serve as two recent examples. Due to the time and courage put forth by the students who work to initiate these GSAs, there are now over 3,000 such groups in schools, and at least one in every state in the United States (Macgillivray, 2007). Whereas students in the United States have had to search for various forms of protection against discrimination based on sexual orientation, Canada has clearly worded provincial and federal human rights codes that offer such protections. In addition to federal protections that exist, some states have non-discrimination laws that can offer students some relief.

5.3.2 State and Local Non-discrimination Laws

State non-discrimination laws that protect individuals based on sexual orientation and/or gender identity only exist in 20 states and the District of Columbia[1] (National Gay and Lesbian Task Force, 2007). However, according to a study published in 2006, only nine states and the District of Columbia (California, Connecticut, Maine, Massachusetts, Minnesota, New Jersey, Vermont, Washington, and Wisconsin) have statutes specifically protecting students in schools from discrimination on the basis of sexual orientation and/or gender identity (Kosciw & Diaz, 2006). Students in these states reported significantly lower rates of verbal harassment than their peers. Since this report, several states' (including Nebraska, Iowa, Kentucky & Wyoming) legislatures have considered bills either expanding or limiting the rights of sexual-minority students (Buchanan, 2006). There are also seven states that have legislation that prohibit the positive portrayal of homosexuality (Alabama, Arizona, Mississippi, Oklahoma, South Carolina, Texas, and Utah), and students in these states reported being verbally harassed at a higher frequency than students from states without such legislation (47.6% as compared to 37.2%) (Kosciw & Diaz, 2006, p. 86).

Two additional cases that were brought before state courts are worth noting here. The first is from the Commonwealth of Massachusetts and the second from the State of New Jersey. The Massachusetts case, *Doe v. Yunits* (2000) is worth discussing as it is one of only two cases found in the research for this book that addresses the realities of transgender youth in schools. In this case, "Pat Doe," a 15-year-old transgender 8th grader, won the right to attend school wearing clothing that expresses her identity as a young woman despite being legally recognized as male. Her principal regularly had sent her home to change her attire and began requiring

---

[1]Minnesota (1993); Rhode Island (1995, 2001); New Mexico (2003); California (1992, 2003); District of Columbia (1997, 2005); Illinois (2005); Maine (2005); Hawaii (1991, 2005, 2006); New Jersey (1992, 2006); Washington (2006); Iowa (2007); Oregon (2007); Vermont (1992, 2007); Colorado (2007); Wisconsin (1982); Massachusetts (1989); Connecticut (1991); New Hampshire (1997); Nevada (1999); Maryland (2001); New York (2002)

her to check with him to have her clothing approved on a daily basis. It was found that the treatment she received from her school principal violated sex discrimination protections provided by the Commonwealth of Massachusetts and that the school could not place restrictions on her attire based on her sex assigned at birth. The Appeals Court supported the lower court's decision to issue an injunction requiring the school to permit Pat to attend, "in clothing and accessories that express her female [sic] gender identity" (*Doe v. Yunits*, 2000, p. 2).

A second case addressing the rights of transgender students in schools was decided by the Maine Human Rights Commission in July 2009 (Curtis, 2009). In this case, a 5th grade student who is legally male, but identifies as a girl, won her claim to allow her to use the girls' restroom at school. The school had previously assigned her to use the staff single-user restroom after she had been harassed by a male peer who followed her in to the girls' restroom and called her "fag." These two state decisions can act as indicators for other schools who are facing the emerging challenges of working with trans youth who are coming out and publicly transitioning while still in the public school system.

The third state decision of interest happened in New Jersey and extended the protections offered by state anti-discrimination laws to cover students in schools. As a result of the complaint brought by a student who had suffered persistent homophobic harassment, the New Jersey Supreme Court held that schools may be held liable under the state Law Against Discrimination for permitting student-on-student bias-based harassment (American Civil Liberties Union-New Jersey, 2007). Chief Justice Zazzali of the N. J. Supreme Court wrote in his decision that "[R]easonable measures are required to protect our youth, a duty that schools are more than capable of performing. . .[W]e require school districts to implement effective preventive and remedial measures to curb severe or pervasive discriminatory mistreatment" (*L.W. v. Toms River Regional Schools Board of Education, A–111–05*, 2007). Hopefully, the requirement that schools take preventive and remedial measures will have far-reaching impacts in schools across New Jersey. These cases provide more examples of how the activism of youth with the support of family and community, will have a significant long-term impact on transforming the climate in schools.

In summary, it should be noted that school districts have not fared well under either federal or state standards. The courts have sided with the youth in most of these cases. The impacts of a toxic school experience for queer youth have been clearly documented in the research literature and are also discussed in Chapter 6. Therefore, it is incumbent upon school districts to take affirmative steps to provide a positive, supportive, and safer school culture for all students. This assumption, however, is not without controversy.

5.4 Safe Schools Policies

As the above listed cases demonstrate, there are legal precedents that exist to protect students from discriminatory behavior in schools. However, many school boards and educators are ignorant of their legal responsibilities and fail to effectively implement and enforce policies that support full equality rights. When they do create inclusive policies, they are often empty promises. As Gerald Walton writes in his article, Bullying and Homophobia in Canadian Schools: The Policies of Policies, Programs, and Educational Leadership, "most school administrators heartily embrace 'safety' but avoid the more challenging but pervasive issues of homophobia, heterosexism, and heteronormativity...in this light, promoting school safety and preventing bullying is largely a public relations exercise" (2004, p. 29). This statement accurately describes the state of policy in many schools. The *Canadian Charter of Rights and Freedoms* was meant to ensure basic human rights for all Canadians and to protect historically marginalized groups from unfair treatment in the public domain. It made important headway in changing cultural attitudes and behaviors to build a more inclusive and proudly diverse society. In *Canada's legal revolution: public education, the Charter, and human rights*, Terri Sussel (1995) asserts that the *Charter's* impact has led to major changes in the field of education. She highlights that case studies show that since the *Charter's* adoption in 1982, legal professionals and the general public have, "tended to have a much higher level of rights consciousness," and that within schools, new policies and practices that address student and employee rights have been adopted (164). In this section, I examine the policies of two exemplary school boards: Vancouver School Board and Toronto District School Board and how they model positive steps toward the meaningful implementation of equality rights for sexual minorities in schools. There are other school districts in Canada and the U.S. that have developed similar policies, but Vancouver and Toronto have highly visible and active BGLQT communities who have advocated for these programs, and as a result, these districts are viewed as leaders in this area. I also discuss how the language and culture established by these policies can have a positive impact on the education of all students in public schools. Based on the above analysis of recent cases, it is important to look at local school policy to understand if and how it reinforces Federal and state or Provincial protections.

5.4.1 Exemplary Inclusive Safe School Policies

Both the Vancouver School Board and the Toronto District School Board have implemented recent policy changes that make them leaders in providing protections and clear implementation steps for confronting homophobia in schools. In a report for the Toronto District School Board, University of Toronto researchers Goldstein, Collins, & Halder asserted that, "in June of 1999 the Toronto District School Board approved perhaps the most comprehensive anti-homophobia policy in North America" (Goldstein, Collins, & Halder, 2005). One of the most promising features of the policy that Goldstein, et al. highlighted was its commitment that the "ideals related to anti-homophobia and sexual orientation equity be reflected in all aspects of organizational structures, policies, guidelines, procedures, classroom practices, day-to-day operations, and communication practices" (Toronto District School Board, 2000). This policy is exemplary because it includes establishing accountability processes as well as allocating resources for policy implementation

(Goldstein et al., 2005). Goldstein and her colleagues do acknowledge some weaknesses in the policy. The main criticism is that it is somewhat vague and not effectively implemented. In their study, they learned that although all TDSB schools are mandated to do some form of anti-homophobia work, many are not doing so. In spite of these criticisms, they conclude that it is "still comprehensive and ground breaking" (Goldstein et al., 2005, p. 13).

A second exemplary school policy is the one implemented by the Vancouver School Board in May 2004. This policy clearly enumerates the individuals protected and the goals of the policy in the following statement:

> The Board will provide a safe environment, free from harassment and discrimination, while also promoting pro-active strategies and guidelines to ensure that lesbian, gay, transgender, transsexual, two-spirit, bisexual and questioning students,(LGBTTQ) employees and families are welcomed and included in all aspects of education and school life and treated with respect and dignity. The purpose of this policy is to define appropriate behaviours and actions in order to prevent discrimination and harassment through greater awareness of and responsiveness to their deleterious effects. This policy is also drafted to ensure that homophobic complaints are taken seriously and dealt with expeditiously and effectively through consistently applied policy and procedures. The policy will also raise awareness and improve understanding of the lives of people who identify themselves on the basis of sexual orientation or gender identity. By valuing diversity and respecting differences, students and staff act in accordance with the Vancouver district's social responsibility initiative (Vancouver School Board, 2004).

The inclusion of *gender identity* along with *sexual orientation* is of note as it serves to strengthen responses to all forms of gendered harassment which are not exclusively homophobic or sexual in nature. In addition to this clear language, the policy includes implementation features that demonstrate institutional support for its effective implementation through all aspects of the school communities. Some of these associated strategies include educating school counselors on queer youth issues, appointing a staff person in each school to be a "safe contact" for students, including curricular resources that positively reflect BGLTQ individuals in the curriculum, offering ongoing staff development in anti-homophobia education, creating partnerships with inclusive organizations and BGLTQ communities, having parent advisory councils that reflect the diversity of the district, and translating information for students and parents into the languages spoken in the home (VSB, 2004). In order for a new policy to be successful, such clear steps must be enumerated and supported by all levels of the school board. It is too early to determine the success of this policy, but the intent and goals listed above give good reason to remain optimistic that it will help improve the experience of queer students and staff in that school board.

In contrast to these two school boards, many other Canadian school policies affirm their support of the Canadian *Charter*, but do not specifically mention or name groups to be protected from discriminatory acts. The importance of including sexual orientation and gender expression as protected classes in school policies cannot be overemphasized. In the absence of this clear language, education professionals tend to err on the side of conservatism and do not effectively intervene in incidents of homophobic harassment. Ian MacGillivray (2003) speaks of the importance of this in his book, *Sexual orientation and school policy: A practical guide for teachers, administrators, and community activists.* In an interview with an American civil rights attorney, he asks, "So do you think it's important to spell out those specific classes?" And the lawyer replies,

> I think it's unfortunate that we've had to go to that length. I don't think anyone thinks it's a great idea that you have to be so specific. But you don't get the government to enforce rights ... unless you're more specific. We had equal rights for a long time but I'm old enough to remember when I was a little kid traveling in the south and there were black and white drinking fountains. They had the same constitution we did. We needed a civil rights act to be passed that you need to extend those equal rights specifically to certain categories and we now know that you can't just say that and have gay, lesbian, and transgendered people be respected because it just hasn't worked. (158)

The strengths of the Vancouver and Toronto policies lie not only in the language, but also in the steps outlined to implement the intent of the policy. Unfortunately, many school boards fall short in offering such protections and proactive strategies for its students, staff, and administrators.

5.4.2 *Implications for Educators*

From the standpoint of protections, it would appear that students in Canadian schools are attending institutions that will protect them from harassment based on sexual orientation (but not gender identity). As this book reveals on closer examination, these protections are tenuous despite the fact that they are explicitly included in many school policies across the United States and Canada. Research indicates that homophobic name-calling and other related forms of harassment are less prevalent in schools and students feel safer in schools that have inclusive bullying and safe schools policies (Kosciw, Diaz, & Greytak, 2008).

Social justice educators and queer youth advocates have reason to be optimistic that the social reforms that have secured greater equality for BGLQT people in Canada will slowly trickle down into practice at the classroom level and expand in schools across the Unites States. Unfortunately, at this time it is only happening in isolated pockets in certain schools and classrooms. Urban areas generally demonstrate increased tolerance and support of sexual diversity and the Vancouver and Toronto School Districts have demonstrated leadership in this area. School districts across North America should look to these districts in order to develop more inclusive policies and practices based on their models.

In studies on bullying and harassment in schools, it has been shown that such behaviors cannot be effectively stopped unless there is a commitment to a cultural change as well as a community-wide effort to write, adopt, and implement a policy and plan of action. In, *Towards bully-free schools: Interventions in action*, Glover, Cartwright, and Gleeson (1998) reported that persuading teachers and administrators of the need for a cultural shift was crucial to the success of anti-bullying policies in the schools. Glover et al. go on to emphasize that, "Where there is not a sense of whole-school ownership of anti-bullying policies, there appears to be less evidence of shared positive values" (p. 58). This sentiment is even more important when addressing such a controversial and complex issue as homophobia. Many teachers and administrators feel unprepared to address issues of sexual orientation and gender expression and as a result are often resistant to such major cultural shifts. In order to truly support equality for all youth in schools, school boards, superintendents, principals, teachers, support staff, parents, and students all need to be included in a coordinated community effort to eradicate this form of discrimination. MacGillivray (2004) noted some of the obstacles one school board in the Unites States faced in effectively implementing such a policy. Some of these barriers include lack of support from top officials, lack of enforcement and effective discipline from principals, lack of knowledge by teachers and support staff of the non-discrimination policy, lack of time and money for publications and training, fear of being targeted for supporting the policy (70–73). These are all concerns that emerged as common themes in my research (Meyer, 2008), and ones that schools must address when working toward successful integration of sexual orientation in their existing safe schools or non-discrimination policies.

Another lesson that can be taken from the United States is from the success stories in the state of Massachusetts. Some of the strategies for success that have been observed in the first state-funded safe schools program for gay, lesbian, bisexual, and transgender youth are shared in the book, *When the drama club is not enough: Lessons from the safe schools program for Gay and Lesbian students.* Perrotti and Westheimer (2001) emphasize the following strategies when working to create safe and inclusive schools for gay, lesbian, and bisexual students: recognize the central role of students, collect and use data effectively, build on the core values of the schools, know the laws and policies that support equity, develop a broad base of support, and create visibility. (20–21)

These successes have been documented in the United States. This is noteworthy since federal protection from discrimination based on sexual orientation does not explicitly exist, and only 14 states have such protections (Cahill & Cianciotto, 2004, p. 14). Often such changes require a large investment of time and money. Although funding can significantly help such efforts, it is important to acknowledge that when there is a commitment from the institution, and a clear position statement from the power structures guiding schools, behaviors will begin to shift to align with those stated ideals. This commitment costs nothing and the benefits are multiple: teachers will feel supported when they send a student to be disciplined for making an anti-gay remark; principals will be role models in keeping the hallways safe from such harassment; bus drivers and cafeteria personnel will help enforce policies effectively when they are clearly informed of their responsibilities. Most educators would agree that it is a priority for their students to feel safe, valued, and supported in schools. To achieve this, the first step that schools must take is to provide a safe learning environment for all students, and that costs nothing.

5.5 Conclusion

Gender and sexual diversity is all around us, although it is often invisible and silenced. Schools cannot make controversies disappear by ignoring them. In many of the legal cases mentioned in this chapter, ignoring the issues exacerbated and escalated the problems. Educators who are responsible for supporting and educating the next generation have a responsibility to create schools and classrooms that value and teach about the diversity that is already present in our communities. Teachers and administrators also have the legal obligation to create safe learning environments that are equitable and free of discrimination. By unlearning the harmful messages repeated through old stereotypes and misinformation, educators have the potential to create and teach more contemporary messages of equality, inclusiveness, and diversity.

References

ACLU. (2004). *Settlement fact sheet: Flores v. Morgan hill unified school district.* Retrieved March 28, 2006, from www.aclu.org

American Civil Liberties Union-New Jersey. (2007). Victory for gay and other students who face harassment. Retrieved October 10, 2007, from http://www.aclu-nj.org/pressroom/ victoryfor-gayandotherstude.htm

Bochenek, M., & Brown, A. W. (2001). *Hatred in the hallways: Violence and discrimination against lesbian, gay, bisexual, and transgender students in U.S. schools*: Human Rights Watch.

Buchanan, W. (2006, April 1). Bills nationwide address gays in schools [Electronic Version]. *SFGate.* Retrieved April 12, 2006, from www.sfgate.com

Cahill, S., & Cianciotto, J. (2004). U.S. Policy Interventions that can make schools safer. *Journal of Gay and Lesbian Issues in Education, 2* (1), 3–16.

Callender, D. R. (2008). When Matt became Jade: Working with a youth who made a gender transition change in high school. In I. Killoran & K. P. Jimenez (Eds.), *Unleashing the unpopular: Talking about sexual orientation and gender diversity in education* (pp. 37–52). Olney, MD: Association for Childhood Education International.

The Canadian Charter of Rights and Freedoms (s. 15). Part I of the Constitution Act c. 11 (1982).

CLE Staff. (2005). BCCA: North Vancouver school board liable for homophobic harassment of student. [Electronic Version]. *Stay current: The continuing legal education society of British Columbia, April 8.* Retrieved April 9, 2005, from www.cle.bc.ca/CLE

Cloud, J. (2005). The battle over gay teens. *Time, October 10.*

Curtis, A. (2009). State rules in favor of young transgender [Electronic Version]. *Bangor Daily News.* Retrieved July 25, 2009, from http://www.bangordailynews.com/detail/109732.html

Dignan, J. (2004, January 8). Important victory for gay students *Gaycitynews.com.* Retrieved October 15, 2007, from http://www.gaycitynews.com/site/index.cfm?newsid= 17008546& BRD=2729&PAG=461&dept_id=568864&rfi=8

Doe v. Bellefonte Area School District (3rd Cir U. S. App. 2004).

Egan v. Canada (2 S.C.R. 513 1995).

Flores v. Morgan Hill Unified School District, No. 02–15128 (9th Cir. 2003).

Goldstein, T., Collins, A., & Halder, M. (2005). *Challenging homophobia and heterosexism in elementary and high schools: A research report to the Toronto district school board.* Toronto, ON: Ontario Instituted for Studies in Education of the University of Toronto.

Harris Interactive. (2001). *Hostile hallways: Bullying, teasing, and sexual harassment in school.* Washington, DC: American Association of University Women Educational Foundation.

Hurley, M. C. (2005). *Sexual orientation and legal rights* (Current Issue Review No. 92–1E). Ottawa, ON: Library of Parliament.

Kempling v. British Columbia College of Teachers (B.C.D. Civ. 2004).

Kosciw, J., & Diaz, E. (2006). *The 2005 national school climate survey: The experiences of lesbian, gay, bisexual and transgender youth in our nation's schools.* New York: Gay, Lesbian, and Straight Education Network.

Kosciw, J., Diaz, E., & Greytak, E. (2008). *2007 National school climate survey: The experiences of lesbian, gay, bisexual, and transgender youth in our nation's schools.* New York, NY: GLSEN.

L.W. v. Toms River Regional Schools Board of Education, A–111–05. (New Jersey Supreme Court 189 N.J. 381, 915 A.2d 535 2007).

Lahey, K. A. (1999). *Are we 'persons' yet? Law and sexuality in Canada.* Toronto, ON: University of Toronto Press.

Lipkin, A. (1999). *Understanding homosexuality, changing schools.* Boulder, CO: Westview Press.

Lugg, C. A. (2006). Thinking about sodomy: Public schools, legal panopticons, and queers. *Educational Policy, 20*(1), 35–58.

Macgillivray, I. K. (2007). *Gay-straight alliances: A handbook for students, educators, and parents.* New York: Harrington Park Press.

Meyer, E. (2007). Lessons from Jubran: Reducing school board liability in cases of peer harassment. *Proceedings of the 17th Annual Conference of the Canadian Association for the Practical Study of Law in Education, 1*, 561–576.

Meyer, E. (2008). Lesbians in popular culture. In C. Mitchell & J. Reid-Walsh (Eds.), *Girl culture: An encyclopaedia* (Vol. 2, pp. 392–394). Westport, CT: Greenwood Press.

Montgomery v. Independent School District No. 709, 109 F. Supp. 2d 1081, 1092 (D. Minn. 2000) 2000).

Nabozny v. Podlesny. (7th Cir. (Wis.) 1996).

National Gay and Lesbian Task Force. (2007, September 17). State nondiscrimination laws in the U.S. Retrieved January 3, 2008, from http://www.thetaskforce.org/downloads/reports/issue_maps/non_discrimination_09_07.pdf

Perrotti, J., & Westheimer, K. (2001). *When the drama club is not enough: Lessons from the safe schools program for gay and lesbian students.* Boston: Beacon Press.

Ray v. Antioch Unified School District. 107 F. Supp. 2d 1165 A.D.Cal. (2000).

School District No. 44 (North Vancouver) v. Jubran, 2005 BCCA 201 (BCSC 6 2005).

Sussel, T. A. (1995). *Canada's legal revolution: Public education, the charter, and human rights.* Toronto, ON: Edmond Montgomery Publications Ltd.

Theno v. Tonganoxie Unified School Dist. No. 464 (2005 WL 3434016 [D. Kan. 2005]).

Trowbridge, C. (2005, December 29). Former student, district settle lawsuit [Electronic Version]. *The tonganoxie mirror.* Retrieved March 16, 2006, from www.tonganoxiemirror.com

Toronto District School Board. (2000). Human Rights Policy (p. 5). Toronto, ON: TDSB.

Trinity Western University v. British Columbia College of Teachers (S.C.R. 772, 2001).

Vancouver School Board. (2004). Lesbian, gay, bisexual, transgender, transsexual, two-spirit, questioning policy. Vancouver, BC.: Vancouver School Board.

Vriend v. Alberta (1 S.C.R. 493 1998).

Walton, G. (2004). Bullying and homophobia in Canadian schools: The politics of policies, programs, and educational leadership. *Journal of Gay and Lesbian Issues in Education, 1*(4), 23–36.

Watkinson, A. (1999). *Education, student rights and the charter.* Saskatoon, SK: Purich.

White County High School Peers in Diverse Education v. White County School District (Civil Action No. 2:06-CV-29-WCO (N. D. Georgia, Gainesville Division). 2006).

Chapter 6
Understanding the Impacts of the School Environment

6.1 Introduction

The problem of ignoring and devaluating gender and sexual diversity in schools is persistent, prevalent, and has long-term tangible harms on many students. Many schools have made attempts at reducing overt violence and harassing behaviors by implementing blanket bullying policies that do little to specifically address the underlying issues of the school climate and culture that allow these behaviors to persist (Soutter & McKenzie, 2000; Walton, 2004). The long-term impacts on individuals targeted for bullying, which include gossip, rumors, and social exclusion, is well documented and severe: lower academic performance, absenteeism, drug and alcohol abuse, and suicidal behaviors (Bond, Carlin, Thomas, Rubin, & Patton, 2001; Rigby & Slee, 1999; Sharp, 1995). Students who are targets of sexual and homophobic harassment have been identified as being at even greater risk for these harmful behaviors and leaving school (California Safe Schools Coalition, 2004; Kosciw & Diaz, 2006; Reis & Saewyc, 1999; Williams, Connolly, Pepler, & Craig, 2005). However, research indicates that schools that have taken positive steps to support gender and sexual diversity and protect students from bullying and harassment can reduce the impact of these negative harms.

This chapter starts by presenting information from research that shows the negative impacts of ignoring gender and sexual diversity in U.S. and Canadian schools and details some of the negative behaviors that emerge from a lack of understanding of and respect for gender and sexual diversity. The second section then details some of the positive impacts of attending a school that has a more positive and inclusive culture toward issues of gender and sexual diversity. The research in this chapter indicates that, in order to foster positive, healthy atmospheres where all students can learn, schools need to address overt discriminatory behaviors as well as more covert types of sexism and heterosexism.

6.2 Understanding Bullying and Harassment

Gendered harassment is a term used to describe any behavior that acts to assert and police the boundaries of traditional gender norms: heterosexual masculinity and

E.J. Meyer, *Gender and Sexual Diversity in Schools*, Explorations of Educational
Purpose 10, DOI 10.1007/978-90-481-8559-7_6, © Springer Science+Business Media B.V. 2010

femininity. It is related to, but different from bullying. Bullying is defined as behavior that repeatedly and over time intentionally inflicts injury on another individual (Olweus, 1993), whereas harassment includes biased behaviors that have a negative impact on the target or the environment (Land, 2003). In other words, bullying is repeated and intentional harms directed at a specific person, whereas harassment is unintentional or intentional behaviors that are discriminatory in nature. Harassing behaviors can be targeted at a specific person, or be general comments or behaviors that are derogatory to an identifiable social group. As a result, it has much broader impacts on the classroom and school culture. Forms of gendered harassment include (hetero)sexual harassment, homophobic harassment, and harassment for gender non-conformity (or transphobic harassment). I link these three forms of harassment because the impacts of the harassers' behavior are linked to the norm setting and policing of the performance of traditional (heterosexual) gender roles (Larkin, 1994; Martino, 1995; Martino & Pallotta-Chiarolli, 2003; Renold, 2002; G. W. Smith & Smith, 1998; Stein, 1995). Although physical bullying is often the most obvious form that is acknowledged and addressed in schools, verbal bullying and harassment are also prevalent and often ignored even though they have been found to be quite damaging to students as well. Hoover and Juul found in their study on bullying that repeated verbal attacks by peers are as devastating as infrequent cases of physical abuse (1993, p. 27). Most bullying policies and interventions are not designed to get at the more persistent and insidious forms of harassment that occur in schools. Canadian researcher Gerald Walton (2004) observes that bullying and zero-tolerance policies, "do not consider the cultural and societal antecedents of violence in schools. Neither do these programs consider *psychological* violence" (p. 29). While I do not wish to ignore the painful experiences that victims of physical harassment and violence endure, it is more likely to be addressed by schools regardless of the assailant's motive. Therefore, this section primarily addresses the more prevalent emotional violence caused by the insidious and ignored issue of gendered harassment that is verbal and psychological in nature.

6.2.1 *Understanding the Scope of the Problem*

I began investigating this problem as a result of my experiences as a high school teacher in the United States observing the hostile climate that existed for BGLQT students in my school. During my first year of teaching I observed a very bright and athletic student – a leader in the school – dissolve into depression, drug use, and skipping classes as a result of how her friends were treating her. She had fallen in love with a young woman she had met that summer and her classmates made sure she felt their disapproval. In addition to being excluded from her peer group, she was verbally harassed on a regular basis. This change in her school experience was enough to send a previously strong and confident young woman into a downward spiral of self-doubt and dangerous behavior. As a young teacher who wanted to support this student, I felt frustrated and angry by what the other teachers allowed to happen in their presence at the school.

As I investigated this problem further, I learned that although BGLQT youth are commonly targeted for harassment, they are not the only ones suffering due to the homophobic and heteronormative climate of the school. Any student whose behavior is perceived to be different in some way can be isolated and harassed using anti-gay insults (O'Conor, 1995; Renold, 2002; Rofes, 1995; Smith & Smith, 1998), and any student who wishes to assert and defend his/her place in the heteronormative social order of the school must engage in heterosexualized discourse which can include various forms of gendered harassment (Duncan, 1999; Martino & Berrill, 2003; Renold, 2003).

Students who are harassed in their schools have been found to be more likely to skip school, abuse drugs and alcohol, and have a higher rate of suicidal ideation (Bagley, Bolitho, & Bertrand, 1997; Irving & Parker-Jenkins, 1995; Rigby & Slee, 1999; Sharp, 1995; Slee, 1995). Most of these students perceive school as a dangerous place which causes significant damage to their level of engagement in the school community. One group of students that is regularly targeted in schools is BGLQT youth (California Safe Schools Coalition, 2004; Kosciw & Diaz, 2006; Reis, 1999; Reis & Saewyc, 1999). In a national phone survey with youth in the United States, the National Mental Health Association (2002) found that 50% of the respondents reported that students who were gay would be bullied most or all of the time. In another U.S. survey, 90% of BGLQT students report hearing homophobic remarks in school frequently or often (Kosciw, Diaz, & Gretytak, 2008). What is disturbing about this trend is not only its prevalence, but the lack of educators' effective intervention to stop this problem. In the Gay, Lesbian, and Straight Education Network (GLSEN) 2007 School Climate Survey, 82% of BGLQT youth say that their teachers rarely or never intervene when hearing homophobic remarks (Kosciw et al., 2008, p. 22). In a study in California, students were asked how often they heard biased remarks (sex, sexual orientation, gender expression, religion, race, disability), and how often teachers intervened. The forms of verbal harassment which students reported hearing the most were based on sexual orientation, race, body size, and gender presentation. The forms that students reported teachers were least likely to interrupt were sexual orientation and gender presentation (California Safe Schools Coalition, 2004) (Fig. 6.1).

These studies indicate that educators are not adequately intervening in these forms of harassment. This inaction on the part of educators teaches students that the institution of the school – and by extension society as a whole – condones such activity. By teaching students that all forms of gendered harassment are tolerated, the institution of the school effectively supports the discriminatory attitudes that cause it to happen in the first place. As democratic institutions in a diverse and changing society, schools must teach about the causes of such harmful attitudes and work to reduce the impacts of them on their students. In so doing, concerned educators and community activists will be able to more effectively work to reduce prejudice and violence in schools. A deeper understanding of different forms of harassment including homophobic harassment, harassment for gender non-conformity (or transphobic harassment), and (hetero)sexual harassment as well the technologies that add

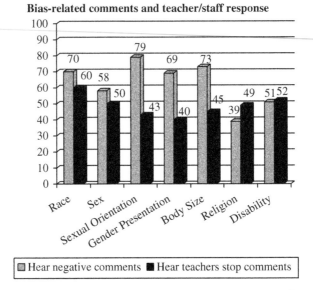

Fig. 6.1 Bias-related comments and teacher/staff response (California Safe Schools Coalition, 2004)

new dimensions to these forms of harassment can better enable educators to engage in this work.

6.2.2 Homophobic Harassment

Homophobic harassment is any behavior, covert or overt, that reinforces negative attitudes toward gay, lesbian, and bisexual people. The most common form of this harassment is verbal in nature and includes the use of anti-gay language as an insult (e.g., "that's so gay" "don't be such a fag"), anti-gay jokes, and behaviors that intend to make fun of gays and lesbians (such as affecting the speech and walk of a stereo-typically effeminate gay man to get a laugh). The prevalence of this discourse in schools allows homophobic attitudes to develop and grow as students learn that this language is tacitly condoned by educators who fail to intervene when it is used. As George Smith explains in his article, *The ideology of "FAG,"*

> The local practices of the ideology of "fag" are never penalized or publicly condemned. Explicitly homophobic ridicule in sports contexts goes unremarked. Effective toleration of the ideology of "fag" among students and teachers condemns gay students to the isolation of "passing" or ostracism and sometimes to a life of hell in school. (1998, p. 332)

This condemnation of gay students in schools is pervasive and damaging. The isolation and vulnerability experienced by these students is exacerbated by the refusal of teachers and administrators to intervene on their behalf. Many students' experiences support Smith's assertion. In the Human Rights Watch (Bochenek & Brown, 2001) study *Hatred in the hallways*, several students spoke of similar experiences:

> Nothing was done by the administration. A guy screamed "queer" down the hall in front of the principal's office, but nothing happened to him. The teachers – yeah, the teachers could have seen what was going on. Nothing happened. (p. 39)
>
> One day in the parking lot outside his school, six students surrounded him. One threw a lasso around his neck, saying, "Let's tie the faggot to the back of the truck." He escaped from his tormentors and ran inside the school. Finding one of the vice-principals, he tried to tell her what had just happened to him. "I was still hysterical," he said, "I was trying to explain, but I was stumbling over my words. She laughed." The school took no action to discipline Dylan's harassers. Instead, school officials told him not to discuss his sexual orientation with other students. After the lasso incident, the harassment and violence intensified. "I was living in the disciplinary office because other harassment was going on. Everyone knew," he said. "It gave permission for a whole new level of physical stuff to occur." (p. 1)

These stories are not exceptional. In GLSEN's National School Climate Survey (Kosciw et al., 2008), 86% of LGBT youth report being verbally harassed in school and 60% report feeling unsafe due to their sexual orientation and 38% felt unsafe because of their gender expression. These students are also targets for school graffiti, vandalism, and ostracism that often leave them at high risk for depression, dropping out of school, and suicide (California Safe Schools Coalition, 2004; GLSEN, 2001; Kosciw et al., 2008; Reis & Saewyc, 1999). On a more positive note, these students report less harassment and increased feelings of school safety when a teacher intervenes sometimes or often to stop name-calling (California Safe Schools Coalition, 2004).

In addition to the risks that BGLTQ youth face in schools as a result of this homophobic climate, students who are perceived to be gender non-conforming are also frequently targeted in schools. Harassment for behavior that transcends narrow gender norms is one that is often mistakenly understood as homophobic harassment, but it is important to discuss as a separate issue so as not to further confuse existing misconceptions of gender identity and expression with sexual orientation.

6.2.3 Harassment for Gender Non-conformity or Transphobic Harassment

Harassment for gender non-conforming behaviors is under-researched, but important to understand. According to the California Safe Schools study, 27% of all students report being harassed for gender non conformity (2004). Due to prevalent stereotypes of gay men and lesbian women who transgress traditional gender norms, people whose behaviors challenge popular notions of masculinity and femininity are often perceived to be gay themselves. This is an incorrect assumption to make as it mistakenly conflates the concepts of sexual orientation and gender identity. Many people engage in this flawed logic due to their misunderstandings of gender and sexual orientation. As explained in earlier chapters, sex, gender identity and expression, and sexual orientation are distinct but interrelated identities and may be

expressed in a variety of ways. For example, although many females (*sex*) identify
as heterosexual (*sexual orientation*) women (*gender identity*), that does not mean
that is the only possible combination of orientations and identities. By allowing
students to engage in this outdated and misinformed way of thinking and behaving,
schools reinforce traditional notions of heterosexual masculinity and femininity that
effectively reduce educational opportunities for all students.

Research has demonstrated that more rigid adherence to traditional sex roles
correlates with more negative attitudes and violent behaviors toward gay men and
lesbians (Bufkin, 1999; Whitley, 2001). When boys disengage from the arts and
girls avoid appearing too athletic, it is often the result of gender stereotypes exert-
ing their powerful influence over the students in the form of teasing and jokes. The
threat of being perceived as a "sissy" or a "tomboy" and the resulting homophobic
backlash limits the ways in which students participate in school life. Martino and
Pallotta-Chiarolli (2003) describe an interview with a student who was harassed for
his interest in art: "On his way to school one morning a group of boys at the back
of the bus from one of the local high schools started calling him names. Initially, he
was targeted as an 'art boy' because he was carrying an art file. But the harassment
escalated and they began calling him 'fag boy'" (p. 52).

Unfortunately, our society's tendency to devalue qualities associated with femininity make this gender performance much harder on non-conforming boys than on
non-conforming girls. Schools tend to place a higher value on strength, competitiveness, aggressiveness, and being tough: qualities generally viewed to be masculine.
Whereas being creative, caring, good at school, and quiet are often considered to
be feminine qualities and are viewed by many as signs of weakness – particularly
in boys. In their study on masculinities in Australian schools, Martino and Pallotta-
Chiarolli (2003) found that "many boys said that while they were able to perform the
techniques of literacy ('I can read'), performing an 'appropriate' masculinity often
prevented or deterred them from displaying their literacy abilities ('I can't read')"
(p. 246). They also discuss how this plays out in physical education: "physically
demanding activities such as dance and gymnastics, where both men and women
excel, are not as esteemed as those sports which serve to provide an arena for the
expression of traditional forms of hegemonic masculinity" (Lingard & Douglas,
1999, cited in Martino & Pallotta-Chiarolli, 2003, p. 254). It is not surprising then
that bullying studies report that "typical victims are described as physically weak,
and they tended to be timid, anxious, sensitive and shy. . . .In contrast, bullies were
physically strong, aggressive, and impulsive, and had a strong need to dominate
others" (Hoover & Juul, 1993, p. 26).

It is difficult to effectively intervene to stop bullying and harassment when the
qualities that perpetrators embody are the ones that are most valued by many and
demonstrate a form of power that is generally esteemed in a patriarchal society.
Hegemonic masculinity (Connell, 1995), the embodiment of the dominant, tough,
competitive, athletic male, is the standard of behavior in schools and any variation
tends to be punished by the peer group (Robinson, 2005; Stoudt, 2006). Though
many researchers understand bullying and harassment as anti-social behavior, the
fact that perpetrators usually hold social power and get what they want out of such

activity shows that they have learned to assert their strength in ways that benefit them. As Walton argues, understanding bullying as anti-social behavior, "is a misconceptualization because it affords dominance and social status and is often rewarded and supported by other children. It may not be nice, but it is, nevertheless, very social" (2004, p. 33). This statement underlines the importance of reconceptualizing how schools are trying to address school safety concerns with generic, oversimplified initiatives to make their schools "bully free." As long as the perpetrators continue to generate social capital (in the form of laughter, attention, and respect from their peers) from their behaviors, a new zero-tolerance policy, a poster, or a one-time guest speaker is not going to have an impact on improving the culture of the school.

The social construct of hegemonic masculinity is at the core of much bullying behavior. As a result of this, students report that schools are safer for gender non-conforming girls (California Safe Schools Coalition, 2004). The pressure on boys to conform to traditional notions of masculinity is great and the risk of being perceived as gay is an effective threat in policing the boundaries of acceptable behavior. One male student described its impacts on his life:

> When I was in elementary school, I did a lot of ballet. I was at the National Ballet School one summer. And that sort of stigma (laugh) which I never thought was a stigma, or could be a stigma, but which became a stigma, followed me into high school. And that was followed with comments continually – "fag," you know, "fag." I think that was actually. . .one of the reasons why I eventually gave up ballet was just because of the constant harassment, and also pursuing other interests. But I think that was at the back of my mind a lot of the time with the harassment, and realizing that they're right. That's what I was. I knew that that's what I was. (Smith & Smith, 1998, p. 322)

This student describes how he eventually gave up his training as a ballet dancer as a result of the stigma that was attached to it by his peers. C.J. Pascoe's (2005, 2007) study of one California school presents an in-depth account of how these practices play out in youth cultures. In her 2005 article, she described the following scene:

> 'There's a faggot over there! There's a faggot over there! Come look!' yelled Brian, a senior at River High School, to a group of 10-year-old boys. Following Brian, the 10 year olds dashed down a hallway. At the end of the hallway Brian's friend, Dan, pursed his lips and began sashaying towards the 10-year-olds. He minced towards them, swinging his hips exaggeratedly and wildly waving his arms. To the boys Brian yelled, 'Look at the faggot! Watch out! He'll get you!' In response the 10-year-olds raced back down the hallway screaming in terror. (Pascoe, 2005, p. 329)

This parody of an effeminate gay male as a threat to young boys is just one of many ways she described observing how the "fag discourse" impacts masculinity and sexuality in schools. When students are limited from developing their strengths because of the climate of the school, then the educational system has failed that student and many others. In order to assert their heterosexual masculinity, many boys engage in overt forms of heterosexualized behaviors as this is seen as the best way to assert one's masculinity and as a result, avoid being called gay. One gay student gave the following example:

You know when all the guys would be making girl jokes, you'd have to go along with them, as much as you tried not to, you still had to chuckle here and there to not raise suspicion…very frequently, jokingly, some students would say to other students – when they didn't necessarily conform to all the jokes and the way of thinking of women students – they'd say, "what, you're not gay, are you?" (Smith & Smith, 1998, p. 324)

In this excerpt, the student explains how he feels obliged to perform a certain kind of masculinity, by participating in the (hetero)sexual harassment of his female peers in order to protect himself from being the target of homophobic harassment. The pressure to participate in these oppressive practices work in multiple ways to assert the power of hegemonic masculinity: it engages additional participants in the sexual harassment of girls and labels those who choose not to participate as gay. This pressure to conform to ideals of hegemonic masculinity is at the core of all three types of gendered harassment outlined in this chapter. This example provides a helpful segue to discuss the third type of gendered harassment: (hetero)sexual harassment.

6.2.4 (Hetero)Sexual Harassment

Sexual harassment in schools has been the subject of research and public discourse since the early 1990s (Corbett, Gentry, & Pearson, 1993; Larkin, 1994; Louis Harris & Associates, 1993; Stein, Linn, & Young, 1992). In spite of this, it is still prevalent in schools. Verbal harassment is the most common form of sexual harassment reported by students and female students experience more frequent and more severe forms of sexual harassment than males (Lee, Croninger, Linn, & Chen, 1996). Terms such as *bitch, baby, chick*, and *fucking broad*, are commonly used in schools by male students as ways to assert masculinity by degrading female peers (Larkin, 1994, p. 268). More recent terms such as *slut, whore*, and *ho*, have been added to this list. Another common way for males to perform their masculinity is to engage in heterosexual discourse by sexually objectifying their female peers and discussing sexual acts they would like to engage in or have already engaged in (Duncan, 1999; Eder, 1997; Larkin, 1994; Stein, 2002). This is often done near the female students, but is not always directed at them, thus creating a space where women are targeted and objectified with no outlet for response or complaint of tangible harm. Such activities create a hostile climate for most students (Stein, 1995; Wood, 1987). This behavior is generally not stopped by teachers, and sometimes it is encouraged by their tacit participation. Students reported that male teachers might, "laugh along with the guys" (Larkin, 1994, p. 270) or support the comments and even blame the victim as demonstrated in the following incident:

I took a photography class, and the majority of the class was boys. … One day I was in the room alone and one of the boys came in. When I went to leave he grabbed me and threw me down and grabbed my breast. I felt I was helpless but I punched him and he ran out. The teacher (who was a man) came in and yelled at me. When I tried to explain why I had hit him the teacher told me I deserved it because I wore short skirts. I was sent to the principal and I had to serve detention. I didn't want to tell the principal because I feared he would do the same and tell me it was my fault. I felt so alone. Everyday I had to go to class and face it. No girl should have to be uncomfortable because of what she wears or how she acts. (Stein, 1995, p. 4)

This example shows how teachers can exacerbate situations by reinforcing the behavior of the offending students. In this case, not only did the teacher not intervene in the sexual harassment, but he added to it by commenting on her attire and stating that she "deserved it." With teachers role modeling and reinforcing such behaviors, it is clear that a new approach to preventing sexual harassment in schools is needed.

Although sexual harassment, by definition, is sexual in nature, I have included it as a form of gendered harassment due to the theoretical understanding of its roots: the public performance of traditional heterosexual gender roles. In its most commonly understood form, sexual harassment is that of a male toward a female and ranges from comments, gestures, leers, or "invitations" of a sexual nature to physical touching, grabbing, rubbing, and violent assault such as rape. I will continue to focus here on the more subtle and insidious behaviors where the harassers attempt to assert social dominance through acts of domination and humiliation, since physically violent and intrusive acts are ones that get a response from school authorities regardless of motive or context.

In Bagley, Bolitho, and Bertrand's (1997) study the researchers used a variety of mental health measures to study the impact of sexual harassment and assault on female students in high schools in Alberta, Canada. They concluded that girls who reported being assaulted "often" were more likely to report emotional disorder and were more than five times as likely to have exhibited suicidal behaviors than were students who were assaulted less frequently or not at all (p. 363). They determined that males are also subjects of sexual harassment; but rates were lower and "the connection with mental health problems is much weaker" (p. 365). More recently, Gruber and Fineran (2008) found that more students experienced bullying (52%) than sexual harassment (34%) and that boys and girls experienced similar levels of both bullying (53 vs. 51%) and harassment (36 vs. 34%). However, they did find a difference in students who identified as gay, lesbian, bisexual, or questioning their sexual orientation (GLBQ). They found that GLBQ students experienced more bullying (79 vs. 50%) and more sexual harassment (71 vs. 32%) than non-GLBQ identified students.

This study also examined the impacts of bullying and sexual harassment on the health of students. They found that girls and GLBQ students generally have poorer health (self-esteem, mental and physical health, and trauma symptoms) during middle and high school. Finally, they concluded that sexual harassment has a more severe impact than bullying on a student's overall health. Their findings led them to conclude that, "the current trend of focusing on [bullying], or else subsuming harassment under bullying, draws attention away from a significant health risk" (Gruber & Fineran, 2008, p. 9) and that schools need to include sexual harassment interventions as a distinct focus.

Related to these deeply embedded gender-related biases in schools is the issue of racism. Both issues are consistently silenced and ignored in spite of their documented negative impacts on students. Although studies show that racial and ethnic harassment is less prevalent than forms of gendered harassment (Kosciw et al., 2008) and that staff are more likely to intervene (California Safe Schools Coalition, 2004; Kosciw et al., 2008), students of color are vulnerable to multiple forms of harassment (Diaz & Kosciw, 2009) and have different experiences of their schools' cultures due to their racial and ethnic group membership. Due to these overlapping and intersecting issues of oppression educators must pay attention to the different needs and experiences of the students in their schools. Each school culture is influenced by the student body, the staff, and the community in which it is situated, therefore these statistics and recommendations need to be adapted by local professionals who have a deep understanding of the local practices and issues in each school community (Meyer, 2008, 2009b).

6.2.5 Cyber-Bullying

Cyber-bullying is defined as "using an electronic medium, such as e-mails or text messages, to threaten or harm others" (Kosciw & Diaz, 2006, p. 27). According to GLSEN's 2005 research, 41% of BGLT students experienced this type of harassment in the past year (Kosciw & Diaz, 2006). This is four times higher than the national average of 9% reported in a recent large-scale study conducted at the University of New Hampshire (Wolak, Mitchell, & Finkelhor, 2006, p. 10). This is not surprising considering that other studies have shown strong links between bullying at school and cyber-bullying. Hinduja and Patchin (2007) found in an online survey that students who were bullies or victims at school were more likely to be involved in cyber-bullying as well. In a Canadian study, Li (2006) also found similarities to school-yard bullying: males (22%) were more likely to be cyber-bullies than females (12%), and males and females reported being victimized online at similar rates (25 vs. 25.6%). Cyber-bullying is a very difficult phenomenon for educators to address since much of it occurs outside of school. However, it is important to recognize that it still has an impact on students' experiences at school (Agatston, Kowalski, & Limber, 2007; Dehue, Bolman, & Vollink, 2008; Smith et al., 2008). Cyber-bullying is somewhat different from school-yard bullying in that it can be anonymous and can have broader impacts with the widespread dissemination of information through broadcast text messages, posted videos, and Web pages. However, these elements can make cyber-bullying easier to prove by documenting the exact nature of the interaction.

This area of bullying research is highly relevant to issues of gendered harassment as researchers have noted that cyberspace is becoming an increasingly hostile environment particularly for girls and BGLQT youth who are targets for harassment online (Barak, 2005; Kosciw & Diaz, 2006; Shariff, 2008). The emergence of new virtual spaces such as discussion boards, blogs, Instant Messaging programs, and social networking sites such as Friendster, Facebook, and MySpace have created new arenas in which youth interact and at times, harass (Jenkins & boyd, 2006). The increasing accessibility of these spaces from Internet-connected laptops, portable gaming devices, and cell phones just multiplies the potential contact points for bullying and harassment. This does not necessarily mean that this is outside the realm of educators' interventions. boyd argues that the visibility and public forum of Internet interactions can actually "provide a window through which teen mentors can help combat [bullying, sexual teasing, and other peer-to-peer harassment]" (Jenkins & boyd, 2006, p. 5). This form of online interaction is an important one for educators and researchers to be aware of as youth behaviors spill out of the school yard and into cyberspace.

6.2.6 Negative Impacts of a Hostile School Environment

In summary, there has been a significant amount evidence collected indicating that schools that have a negative climate and silence issues related to gender and sexual diversity have a negative impact on many aspects of students' lives: academics, school and community engagement, as well as their emotional and physical well-being. The most recent National School Climate Survey conducted by GLSEN (Kosciw et al., 2008) provides data that clearly outline that students who are frequent victims of forms of gendered harassment have lower GPAs and are less likely to plan to pursue post-secondary education. These students are also more likely to skip school due to reasons of personal safety. This chronic absenteeism due to fears for personal safety can cause students to disengage from school activities and eventually drop out.

As noted above, many studies have pointed out the harmful impacts that bullying and harassment in schools can have on the on emotional and physical well-being of BGLQT and gender non-conforming youth. Negative emotional impacts include depression, loneliness, and suicidal ideation (D'Augelli et al., 2005). These are also related to physical health risks including drug and alcohol abuse (Grossman & D'Augelli, 2005), engaging in high-risk sexual behaviors, and suicide (Reis & Saewyc, 1999). Additionally, students in school environments that are hostile to gender and sexual diversity may be at higher risk for physical and sexual assault due to their sex, sexual orientation, or gender identity and expression (Kosciw et al., 2008; National Mental Health Association, 2002; Williams, Connolly, Pepler, & Craig, 2003).

In spite of all of these potential hazards, there are some encouraging findings as well. BGLQT students report greater feelings of school safety, fewer homophobic remarks, and more effective faculty interventions in schools that have comprehensive policies (GLSEN, 2008, p. 125). GLSEN also reported that in states that had comprehensive laws protecting GLBT students from harassment, students reported fewer homophobic remarks, more faculty intervention, and lower levels of harassment and assault (GLSEN 2008, p. 129). Finally, students who see teachers stop negative comments and slurs based on sexual orientation, report less name-calling and stronger feelings of school safety. These are important findings as they demonstrate the impact that effective interventions can have on the experiences of students in schools (California Safe Schools Coalition, 2004, p. 19). These findings suggest that positive school environments have the potential to reverse, or possibly eliminate, the effects of negative schooling experiences.

6.3 Impacts of a Positive School Environment

Although there are many schools across North America that have hostile climates toward gender and sexual diversity and actively attempt to silence any educational or supportive dialogue around these issues, there are schools that are taking proactive steps to create inclusive learning environments that celebrate the diversity and contributions of all members of their school communities. With ongoing efforts to improve the graduation rates and academic performance of students from public schools, it is important to learn from the successes of schools that have demonstrated success in teaching about gender and sexual diversity. Schools that have anti-harassment and non-discrimination policies, inclusive curricula, and supportive staff can have a significant positive impact on the experiences of students and their families (Kosciw et al., 2008) including in the areas of academics, school and community engagement, and emotional and physical well-being.

6.3.1 Academics

Schools that work to create positive school climates regarding gender and sexual diversity have shown greater levels of academic success for BGLQT students. Several of the areas of positive impact in the area of academics include increased feelings of school safety which likely lead to better attendance, higher GPAs, and more perseverance on to higher education (Kosciw et al., 2008). In addition to creating safer school environments through policy initiatives, diversifying the curriculum is another important step to address gender and sexual diversity. In GLSEN's 2007 National School Climate Survey, the researchers documented that schools with curricula that included issues related to gender and sexual diversity had fewer reports of homophobic remarks, harassment and assault, and increased feelings of school safety and belonging. This report also demonstrated that when educators effectively intervened in incidents of gendered harassment, there was decreased absenteeism due to safety concerns. GLBT students who were able to identify at least one supportive educator in their school had higher GPAs and educational aspirations than those who did not have such an ally in their school. What these data tell us is that in order for students to achieve academically and to choose to continue their education during and beyond high school, they need to have positive and supportive educational experiences. Many youth have the ability to excel; however, some may disengage from academics due to feelings of alienation, frustration, and being misunderstood or ignored by their teachers and administrators. In order to ensure the best chance of academic success for all, schools can do more to meet the needs of their students.

6.3.2 School and Community Engagement

Positive school climates can also strengthen students' overall engagement with school (Ryan & Patrick, 2001). Students who are involved in extracurricular activities have a stronger connection to the school community and tend to perform better academically (Fredericks, Blumenfeld, & Paris, 2004). Gay–Straight Alliances and other such clubs are one example of an extracurricular activity that can help create a positive school experiences for BGLQT youth and children in BGLQT-parented families. In an article published in 2003, Laura Szlacha reported results from her study of Massachusetts schools who implemented aspects of the Safe Schools Program for Gay and Lesbian Students (Massachusetts Department of Education, 2007). This program was the first statewide initiative to address homophobia in schools and required schools to revise policies, provide staff training, and support the creation of student-led associations in order to improve the experiences of BGLQT students. Her study found that having a student Gay–Straight Alliance, "is the aspect most strongly associated with positive sexual diversity climates"(p. 73). Students in schools with GSAs report less homophobic remarks, less harassment and assault, and increased feelings of school safety and school belonging (Kosciw et al., 2008, p. 114). In addition to providing students a forum to safely discuss issues relating to gender and sexual diversity, GSAs can help provide students valuable leadership opportunities. Gay–Straight Alliances and related groups are available in thousands of high schools across the United States and Canada and more are forming every year (Macgillivray, 2007; Meyer, 2009a). Although these groups are not without controversy, Chapter 5 addressed the legal issues that are involved if a school tries to prevent students from starting such an organization.

A second way that schools can create more positive learning environments is by providing students with meaningful leadership opportunities. In a study of BGLQT students on college and university campuses, Renn and Bilodeau (2005) reported that experiences in positions of leadership offered students important opportunities to connect with the community, learn valuable advocacy skills, and negotiate a stronger sense of identity. Their study focused on students who were leaders of organizations that had a focus on BGLQT students and their concerns.

A third way that schools can help provide a positive learning environment is to encourage faculty and staff who may identify as BGLQT to be open about this aspect of their identity in order for students to learn that it is safe and valued to be BGLQT and "out" in their school. Many schools have an unwritten "don't ask, don't tell" policy that is clearly recognizable to community members. By not allowing adults to be out, students learn that it is an aspect of identity that is not valued or recognized and should be concealed. This is how shame and self-hate are learned. Although it is not always possible for teachers to come out in their communities for reasons of safety or job security, in her research with gay and lesbian teachers, Janna Jackson (2007) found that teachers noticed a reduction in verbal name-calling after they came out at school. Having adult role models can help students feel more confident to divulge that they have a BGLQT parent, sibling, or even come out themselves. Students who felt comfortable being out in their schools report feeling more connected to and supported by their school community (Kosciw et al., 2008, p. 91). This sense of belonging is important for student achievement and overall well-being, which is addressed more fully in the next section.

6.3.3 Emotional and Physical Well-Being

Emotional and physical well-being are also impacted by school climate. Just as a poisonous school climate can damage a student both physically and emotionally, a positive school climate can offer students a safe place to (1) learn about relationships, (2) establish a stronger sense of self, and (3) learn to appreciate all forms of diversity. These three areas and their implications for student's overall physical mental health are addressed in this section.

Schools are the center of most students' social universe and are the site of important friendships, crushes, and dating relationships. During high school, adolescents learn to adapt the rules of friendship as they mature and the interests and needs of their friends shift and grow. They learn to balance the demands of both friends and romantic interests, and how to navigate the difficult steps of initiating and maintaining a dating relationship. In a positive school climate, students are provided a social network of supportive peers and adults to observe, talk to, and learn from. During adolescence the peer group has the most important influence on a person; therefore it is important that students feel that they can be their whole selves in their relationships at school. Schools also can provide accurate and life-saving information about relationships and safer sexual practices. Sadly, many schools offer abstinence-only or a heteronormative sexual education curriculum. However, schools that do offer information that is relevant to students' lives can provide valuable guidance and support to adolescents as they learn to establish, build, and negotiate relationships. Providing students balanced and accurate information about dating, emotional and physical intimacy, and making choices about sexual behaviors can help teens make more informed, healthier choices for themselves and their partners. In order to develop healthy relationships, students also need to establish a strong sense of self.

Adolescence is a period of identity development when many youth are exploring and learning more about who they want to be. Schools that provide an open and supportive environment for students to fully embrace the aspects of themselves that make them feel proud, accomplished, creative, and successful are places where all students will succeed. In order for students to develop this self-awareness and self-esteem they need diverse role models, a safe learning environment, and multiple opportunities to explore and identify their strengths and passions. Many students are deterred from their interests in schools due to narrow expectations based on gender roles. However, if students learn that they are valued for their contributions whether they are artistic, athletic, academic, vocational, traditional or hi-tech, then they will develop a healthier sense of self and a greater appreciation for others.

Appreciation for diversity is an important lesson that students in our multicultural and changing world need to learn. With increased mobility and the impacts of the global economy, immigration patterns are shifting and the United States and

Canada are growing increasingly culturally, linguistically, religiously, and ethnically diverse. Schools that provide a positive school environment regarding gender and sexual diversity are also providing students with valuable lessons with regards to all these other forms of diversity. In order to prepare students to be active and engaged citizens in a pluralistic, democratic society, schools can offer models of how to resolve conflicts, learn across differences, and gain strength from diverse perspectives and ideas. By teaching the lessons of recognizing and valuing difference and creating a school environment that embraces and celebrates the diversity of their community, educators can help reduce prejudice and promote understanding. These lessons can have long-term positive impacts on the life of a student and a community.

6.4 Conclusion

The climate of a school can have a greater and longer-lasting impact on students' lives than the official curriculum; however, it is often overlooked. It infuses all aspects of students' experiences: physical and emotional safety, academic and personal success, motivation and engagement, as well as whether they feel visible and valued by the peers and teachers. There has been much research in the past decade that illuminates the physical and emotional tolls that negative school environments have on BGLQT youth and families. In addition to being targeted for various forms of bullying and harassment, negative school climates can cause students to disengage from school both academically and physically by skipping classes or dropping out. It can lead teens to self-harming behaviors such as abusing drugs and alcohol, engaging in high-risk sexual activities, and attempting suicide. Although negative school climates are harmful in many ways, a result of negative school climates, many BGLQT youth are very resilient and manage to survive and thrive in spite of the hostility they experience at school.

All schools are not so harmful. Some schools have taken proactive measures to revise bullying and harassment policies, provide educational resources, and offer training to their faculty and staff on issues of gender and sexual diversity. Other schools and individual teachers have worked actively to include BGLQT topics in the curriculum and support extracurricular activities and clubs that address homophobia, heterosexism, and transphobia. Schools that have taken these steps are providing positive learning environments for all students that can lead to improved academic performance, perseverance in school, and increased feelings of school safety and engagement. Schools that work to actively include and value gender and sexual diversity are places where all students and families can see themselves and where everyone has an opportunity to succeed.

This chapter has provided a broad overview of the negative and positive impacts that the climate of the school can have on students' experiences and chances at future success. In order to reduce the potential risks of dropping out, drug abuse, and suicide, schools can take clear steps to provide a positive learning environment. This supportive school culture can provide students a place to identify and capitalize on their strengths, develop healthy relationships, establish a stronger sense of self and learn to appreciate diversity in all its forms. The last chapter offers guidance on how to improve school cultures to maximize the learning and development of all students.

References

Agatston, P. W., Kowalski, R., & Limber, S. (2007). Students' perspectives on cyber bullying. *Journal of Adolescent Health, 41*(6, suppl), S59–S60.

Bagley, C., Bolitho, F., & Bertrand, L. (1997). Sexual assault in school, mental health and suicidal behaviors in adolescent women in Canada. *Adolescence, 32*(126), 361–366.

Barak, A. (2005). Sexual harassment on the internet. *Social Science Computer Review, 23*(1), 77–92.

Bochenek, M., & Brown, A. W. (2001). *Hatred in the hallways: Violence and discrimination against lesbian, gay, bisexual, and transgender students in U.S. schools.* New York: Human Rights Watch.

Bond, L., Carlin, J. B., Thomas, L., Rubin, K., & Patton, G. (2001). Does bullying cause emotional problems? A prospective study of young teenagers. *BMJ: British Medical Journal, 323*(7311), 480–484.

Bufkin, J. L. (1999). Bias crime as gendered behavior. *Social Justice, 26*(1), 155–176.

California Safe Schools Coalition. (2004). *Consequences of harassment based on actual or perceived sexual orientation and gender non-conformity and steps for making schools safer.* Davis: University of California.

Connell, R. W. (1995). *Masculinities.* Sydney: Allen and Unwin.

Corbett, K., Gentry, C. A., & Pearson, W. J. (1993). Sexual harassment in high school. *Youth & Society, 25*(1), 93–103.

D'Augelli, A. R., Grossman, A. H., Salter, N. P., Vasey, J. J., Starks, M. T., & Sinclair, K. O. (2005). Predicting the suicide attempts of lesbian, gay and bisexual youth. *Suicide and Life-Threatening Behavior, 35*(6), 646–660.

Dehue, F., Bolman, C., & Vollink, T. (2008). Cyberbullying: Youngsters' experiences and parental perception. *CyberPsychology & Behavior 11*(2), 217–223.

Diaz, E., & Kosciw, J. (2009). *Shared differences: The experiences of lesbian, gay, bisexual, and transgender students of color in our Nation's schools.* New York, NY: GLSEN.

Duncan, N. (1999). *Sexual bullying: Gender conflict and pupil culture in secondary schools.* London: Routledge.

Eder, D. (1997). Sexual aggression within the school culture. In B. Bank & P. M. Hall (Eds.), *Gender, equity, and schooling* (pp. 93–112). London: Garland Publishing.

Fredericks, J., Blumenfeld, P., & Paris, A. (2004). School engagement: Potential of the concept, state of the evidence. *Review of Educational Research, 74*(1), 59–109.

GLSEN. (2001). *The national school climate survey: Lesbian, gay, bisexual and transgender youth and their experiences in schools.* New York, NY: The Gay, Lesbian, and Straight Education Network.

Grossman, A. H., & DAugelli, A. R. (2005). Recreational substance use among gay, lesbian, and bisexual youth: Frequency and predictors. In P. Bramham & J. Caudwell (Eds.), *Sport, active leisure and youth cultures* (pp. 55–72). Eastbourne: LSA Publications.

Gruber, J. E., & Fineran, S. (2008). Comparing the impact of bullying and sexual harassment victimization on the mental and physical health of adolescents. *Sex Roles, 59*, 1–13.

Hinduja, S., & Patchin, J. W. (2007). Offline consequences of online victimization: School violence and delinquency. *Journal of School Violence, 6*(3), 89–112.

Hoover, J. H., & Juul, K. (1993). Bullying in Europe and the United States. *Journal of Emotional and Behavioral Problems, 2*(1), 25–29.

Irving, B. A., & Parker-Jenkins, M. (1995). Tackling truancy: An examination of persistent non-attendance amongst disaffected school pupils and positive support strategies. *Cambridge Journal of Education, 25*(2), 225–235.

Jackson, J. (2007). *Unmasking Identities: An exploration of the lives of gay and lesbian teachers.* Lanham, MD: Lexington Books.

Jenkins, H., & boyd, d. (2006). Discussion: Myspace and Deleting Online Predators Act (DOPA) [Electronic Version]. *Digital divide network.* Retrieved May 31, 2006, from www.digitaldivide.net/articles

Kosciw, J., & Diaz, E. (2006). *The 2005 national school climate survey: The experiences of lesbian, gay, bisexual and transgender youth in our nation's schools.* New York, NY: The Gay, Lesbian and Straight Education Network.

Kosciw, J., Diaz, E., & Gretytak, E. (2008). *2007 National School Climate Survey: The experiences of lesbian, gay, bisexual, and transgender youth in our nation's schools.* New York, NY: GLSEN.

Land, D. (2003). Teasing apart secondary students' conceptualizations of peer teasing, bullying and sexual harassment *School Psychology International, 24*(2), 147–165.

Larkin, J. (1994). Walking through walls: The sexual harassment of high school girls. *Gender and Education, 6*(3), 263–280.

Lee, V., Croninger, R. G., Linn, E., & Chen, Z. (1996). The culture of sexual harassment in secondary schools. *American Educational Research Journal, 33*(2), 383–417.

Li, Q. (2006). Cyberbullying in schools: A research of gender differences. *School Psychology International, 27*(2), 157–170.

Louis Harris & Associates. (1993). *Hostile hallways: The AAUW survey on sexual harassment in America's schools* Washington, DC: American Association of University Women.

Macgillivray, I. K. (2007). *Gay-straight alliances: A handbook for students, educators, and parents.* Binghamton, NY: Harrington Park Press.

Martino, W. (1995). 'Cool boys', 'party animals', 'squids' and 'poofters': Interrogating the dynamics and politics of adolescent masculinities in school. *British Journal of Sociology of Education, 22*(2), 239–263.

Martino, W., & Berrill, D. (2003). Boys, schooling and masculinities: Interrogating the 'Right' way to educate boys. *Educational Review, 55*(2), 99–117.

Martino, W., & Pallotta-Chiarolli, M. (2003). *So what's a boy? Addressing issues of masculinity and schooling.* Buckingham, : Open University Press.

Massachusetts Department of Education. (2007, November 20). The Safe Schools Program for Gay & Lesbian Students. Retrieved December 17, 2007, from http://www.doe.mass.edu/cnp/safe/ssch.html

Meyer, E. J. (2008). Gendered harassment in secondary schools: Understanding teachers' (non)interventions. *Gender & Education, 20*(6), 555–572.

Meyer, E. J. (2009a). Book Review Essay: Handbooks for educators working with Gay-Straight Alliances. *Journal of GLBT Youth, 6*(3/4), 317–324.

Meyer, E. J. (2009b). *Gender, bullying, and harassment: Strategies to end sexism and homophobia in schools.* New York: Teachers College Press.

National Mental Health Association. (2002). *What does gay mean? Teen survey executive summary.* Alexandria, VA: National Mental Health Association.

O'Conor, A. (1995). Who gets called queer in school? Lesbian, gay, and bisexual teenagers, homophobia, and high school. In G. Unks (Ed.), *The Gay teen: Educational practice and theory for lesbian, gay, and bisexual adolescents* (pp. 95–104). New York: Routledge.

Olweus, D. (1993). *Bullying at school: What we know and what we can do.* Oxford: Blackwell Publishing.

Pascoe, C. J. (2005). 'Dude, You're a Fag': Adolescent masculinity and the fag discourse. *Sexualities, 8*(3), 329.

Pascoe, C. J. (2007). *Dude, you're a fag: Masculinity and sexuality in high school.* Berkeley, CA: University of California Press.

Reis, B. (1999). *They don't even know me: Understanding anti-gay harassment and violence in schools*. Seattle, WA: Safe Schools Coalition of Washington.

Reis, B., & Saewyc, E. (1999). *83,000 Youth: Selected findings of eight population-based studies*. Seattle, WA: Safe Schools Coaltion of Washington.

Renn, K. A., & Bilodeau, B. (2005). Queer student leaders: An exploratory case study of identity development and LGBT student involvement. *Journal of Gay and Lesbian Issues in Education, 2*(4), 49–72.

Renold, E. (2002). Presumed innocence – (Hetero)sexual, heterosexist and homophobic harassment among primary school girls and boys. *Childhood – A global journal of child research, 9*(4), 415–434.

Renold, E. (2003). 'If you don't kiss me you're dumped': Boys, boyfriends and heterosexualised masculinities in the primary school. *Educational Review, 55*(2), 179–194.

Rigby, K., & Slee, P. (1999). Suicidal ideation among adolescent school children, involvement in bully-victim problems, and perceived social support. *Suicide and Life-Threatening Behavior, 29*(2), 119–130.

Robinson, K. H. (2005). Reinforcing hegemonic masculinities through sexual harassment: issues of identity, power and popularity in secondary schools. *Gender and Education, 17*(1), 19–37.

Rofes, E. (1995). Making our schools safe for sissies. In G. Unks (Ed.), *The gay teen: Educational practice and theory for Lesbian, Gay, and Bisexual Adolescents* (pp. 79–84). New York: Routledge.

Ryan, A., & Patrick, H. (2001). The Classroom social environment and changes in adolescents' motivation and engagement during middle school. *American Educational Research Journal, 38*(2), 437–460.

Shariff, S. (2008). *Cyberbullying: Issues and solutions for the school, the classroom and the home*. New York: Routledge.

Sharp, S. (1995). How much does bullying hurt? The effects of bullying on the personal well being and educational progress of secondary aged students. *Educational & Child Psychology, 12*(2), 81–88.

Slee, P. (1995). Bullying: Health concerns of Australian secondary school students. *International Journal of Adolescence & Youth, 5*(4), 215–224.

Smith, G. W., & Smith, D., Ed. (1998). The ideology of "fag": The school experience of gay students. *Sociological Quarterly, 39*(2), 309–335.

Smith, P. K., Mahdavi, J., Carvalho, M., Fisher, S., Russell, S., & Tippett, N. (2008). Cyberbullying: Its nature and impact in secondary school pupils. *Journal of Child Psychology and Psychiatry, 49*(4), 376–385.

Soutter, A., & McKenzie, A. (2000). The use and effects of anti-bullying and anti-harassment policies in Australian schools. *School Psychology International, 21*(1), 96–105.

Stein, N. (1995). Sexual harassment in school: The public performance of gendered violence. *Harvard Educational Review, 65*(2), 145–162.

Stein, N. (2002). Bullying as sexual harassment in elementary schools. In E. Rassen (Ed.), *The Jossey-Bass reader on gender in education* (pp. 409–429). San Francisco: Jossey-Bass.

Stein, N., Linn, E., & Young, J. (1992). Bitter lessons for all: Sexual harassment in schools. In J. T. Sears (Ed.), *Sexuality and the curriculum* (pp. 149–174). New York,: Teachers College Press.

Stoudt, B. G. (2006). You're either in or you're out: School violence, peer discipline, and the (re)production of hegemonic masculinity. *Men And Masculinities, 8*(3), 273–287.

Szlacha, L. (2003). Safer sexual diversity climates: Lessons learned from an evaluation of Massachusetts safe schools program for gay and lesbian students. *American Journal of Education, 110*(1), 58–88.

Walton, G. (2004). Bullying and homophobia in Canadian schools: The politics of policies, programs, and educational leadership. *Journal of Gay and Lesbian Issues in Education, 1*(4), 23–36.

Whitley, B. E., Jr. (2001). Gender-role variables and attitudes toward homosexuality. *Sex Roles,* *45*(11/12), 691–721.

Williams, T., Connolly, J., Pepler, D., & Craig, W. (2003). Questioning and sexual minority adolescents: High school experiences of bullying, sexual harassment and physical abuse. *Canadian Journal of Community Mental Health, 22*(2), 47–58.

Williams, T., Connolly, J., Pepler, D., & Craig, W. (2005). Peer victimization, social support, and psychosocial adjustment of sexual minority adolescents. *Journal of Youth and Adolescence, 34*(5), 471–482.

Wolak, J., Mitchell, K., & Finkelhor, D. (2006). *Online victimization of youth: Five years later.* Durham, NH: The Crimes against Children Research Center, University of New Hampshire.

Wood, J. (1987). Groping towards sexism: Boys' sex talk. In M. Arnot & G. Weiner (Eds.), *Gender under scrutiny: New inquiries in education* (pp. 187–230). London: Hutchinson Education.

Chapter 7
Transforming School Cultures

7.1 Introduction

This book was written to help current and future educators, including school counselors and administrators to better understand issues of gender and sexual diversity in order to improve the way these issues are addressed in schools. As Chapter 6 points out, there are many long-term negative impacts on all students and families when local schools allow persistent and systemic homophobia, sexism, heterosexism, and transphobia to pervade classrooms, hallways, gyms, and other learning environments. In order to help readers apply the concepts introduced in this volume to their specific professional contexts, this chapter presents specific approaches to transforming school cultures to be more inclusive of gender and sexual diversity.

As mentioned earlier, there are many factors that influence school culture and this chapter breaks down these multiple influences into subcategories that assist readers in assessing the needs of a specific school community and how best to address those needs. The discussion of how to read one's school culture is followed by a series of recommendations of tangible steps to take in order to transform these environments. The third section identifies potential challenges and sites of resistance to this work in schools and offers suggestions to surmount those challenges. Finally, this chapter concludes with a list of Web resources, books, and videos that can provide support to assist readers working to transform their school's culture.

7.2 Understanding School Cultures

In order to understand the multiple influences that shape how a school addresses and responds to issues related to sexual and gender diversity, I designed a theoretical model based on my research with teachers on these issues (Meyer, 2008a). I have developed a diagram to illustrate this model that shows the various forces that influence school cultures and educators' roles in shaping it (Fig. 7.1).

There are four tiers to this model that demonstrate the relationship between the main factors that influence how teachers perceive and respond to gender and sexual diversity in school: external influences, internal influences, perceptions of

E.J. Meyer, *Gender and Sexual Diversity in Schools*, Explorations of Educational Purpose 10, DOI 10.1007/978-90-481-8559-7_7, © Springer Science+Business Media B.V. 2010

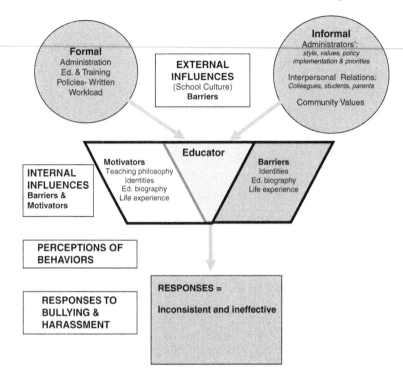

Fig. 7.1 Factors influencing school cultures

behaviors, and responses to behaviors. As the diagram shows, there are two categories of external influences (formal and informal) that get filtered through the teachers' internal influences (philosophy, identities, educational biography, and life experiences). This interaction of external and internal influences shapes their perceptions of and responses to student behaviors. The two categories that form the external influences are formal and informal.

7.2.1 External Influences

Formal influences are the most explicit of the external forces that help shape school cultures and include administrative structures, school policies, teacher education, and curriculum, and workload demands. These factors interact with informal influences to shape educators' experiences of the school culture. Informal influences include the accepted norms and values in the school community and are absorbed from superiors (administration), peers (colleagues), students, and families/community members.

In my research, the informal influence of administrators was significant in impacting how and when teachers chose to intervene in incidents of gendered harassment. This administrative influence included several aspects of school leadership that went beyond policy and job description and included administrators' style, personal values, professional priorities, and policy implementation. In other words, the way in which principals and vice-principals chose to lead their school had possibly greater impact than the stated policies and procedures of the school and school district. This was communicated through the choices principals make about how to spend professional development time, what policies to highlight and enforce, what teachers and students to recognize and reward, and how others might be singled out and informally "punished" with difficult schedules, extra surveillance, or undesirable assignments. Other aspects of the informal school culture that impact students' and teachers' experiences included colleagues' approaches to teaching and enforcing rules as well as the values embraced and endorsed by the student body and the surrounding community that were prevalent in the school. The interaction between the external influences and internal influences can explain the wide variety of perceptions of and responses to gender and sexual diversity issues by educators.

Both external and internal influences present barriers and motivators to educators' efforts to create schools that value diversity. These influences vary based on teachers' identities and experiences in their school cultures, but in most cases in this study, the barriers outweigh the motivators to take steps toward a positive transformation of school cultures. The teachers in my research reported that every aspect of these external influences communicated to them that sexism, homophobia, and transphobia were accepted and endorsed in their school communities, and proactive responses against these forms of bias were not supported. This imbalance creates a constant struggle for the educators who are trying to reduce such harmful behaviors in their classrooms and schools but face constant institutional resistance.

7.2.2 Institutional Resistance

The data collected in my study (Meyer, 2008a, 2009) and other related projects (Goodenow, Szalacha, & Westhimer, 2006; Greytak & Kosciw, 2008; Kosciw, Diaz, & Gretytak, 2008; Macgillivray, 2004; Perrotti & Westheimer, 2001; Stader & Graca, 2007; Thonemann, 1999) support three forms of resistance Britzman (2000) identified to addressing topics related to sexuality in schools: structural, pedagogical, and psychical. Research shows that external factors create a majority of the barriers to effective intervention in cases of gendered harassment. Both formal and informal structures work together to prevent effective education and responses to bias and silence around issues of sex, gender, and sexuality. The first form of resistance identified by Britzman is structural resistance, which she defines as "the very design or organization of education" (p. 34). Sources of structural resistance include administrators' style, policy implementation, and teacher workload demands. The second form of resistance Britzman identifies is pedagogical, which she breaks into two types: "one direction worries about Eros between students and teachers. Another direction considers sexuality as the secret of an individual's nature" (p. 34). Examples of such barriers include teacher education and training that is silent about gender and sexual diversity and state or provincial curricula that clearly exclude discussions about non-dominant genders and sexualities or do not explicitly create expectations or pedagogical support materials to teach inclusively about these issues.

The third form of resistance is psychical, which Britzman explains as "the conflict within" (p. 34). Psychical resistance is most commonly found in administrators' and other teachers' personal values that are often rooted in traditional cultural or religious notions about gender roles and sexuality. These personal belief systems validate and perpetuate the status quo. Conversely, the teachers in my study, and many others like them, have internal influences that encourage them to work through resistance, such as their educational biographies, personal identities, and teaching philosophies, that motivated them to do their best to challenge gendered harassment in spite of the many formal and informal barriers in their schools (Meyer, 2008a, 2008b). Educators' internal influences are strong factors that shape their practice in schools and can be powerful motivators to work through forms of external resistance. The next section addresses these influences.

7.2.3 Internal Influences

The teachers in my research all spoke of a deep awareness of and commitment to addressing incidents of bias in their classrooms. If teachers do not have educational biographies or teaching philosophies that help them gain an awareness of racism, sexism, transphobia, homophobia, and other forms of bias, they may have fewer internal motivators to induce them to intervene. Additionally, if teachers hold personal values that do not support equality rights based on sex, sexual orientation, and gender identity or expression then their internal influences would act as additional barriers to confronting acts of gendered harassment and reproduction of heteronormativity when they occur. It is for this reason that teacher education and school leadership programs must work to include a deeper understanding of all kinds of diversity and equity issues; especially those related to sex, gender, and sexuality so that they may increase their awareness of and attention to these issues in schools. In addition to preparing teachers to offer instruction in their subject areas, these programs must encourage educators to think critically and reflect on their own identities and biases in order to better prepare them for working in increasingly diverse school communities.

Through the process of listening to teachers talk about their experiences with gendered harassment in schools, it became clear that it would not be possible for them to teach inclusively on issues related gender and sexual diversity until a shift in the entire school culture occurred. They spoke about anti-gay jokes by their principals, sexual harassment perpetrated by their colleagues, and a general acceptance of sexist and homophobic language throughout the school.

7.3 Engaging the Whole School Community

While overt acts of discrimination are difficult for schools to ignore, daily acts of covert discrimination persist and impact students' lives in ways that many teachers and administrators fail to acknowledge. When bias against an identifiable social group is present throughout an institution, the entire school is implicated and the culture must shift. In order to transform ignorance of and intolerance for forms of sexual diversity, all stakeholders in the community must be involved in the process: students, families, teachers, administrators and school board personnel. The tone must be set by the leadership, but everyone must be engaged in changing the culture of the institution. In order to better identify what steps can be taken at each level, recommendations are provided for the following groups: administrators and school boards, teachers and support staff, students, parents, and community members.

For each one of these groups, change must first begin at the personal level. Before anyone can begin working collectively to improve school climates, all individuals must take responsibility for confronting their own biases and blind spots by actively educating themselves around issues that they may be under-informed or uncomfortable with. Such education can include reading books, searching information on the Internet, viewing films, or attending public lectures and workshops. It can also be extended to participating in interactive activities such as online discussion groups, graduate coursework, or joining or initiating a community group or task force to focus on these issues. Beyond the personal level, there are several institutional and community actions that also can be taken.

7.3.1 Administrators and School Boards

At the school leadership level, important changes must be made in three areas to set the tone for a positive and supportive school environment. These are policy, education, and resources and support. Without the institutional support provided by the following examples, the isolated efforts of overworked teachers, frustrated parents, and targeted young people will only have a small, short-term impact on the experiences of the students in the school community. In order to have a larger, more lasting effect on the school culture, systemic changes must be made.

Policy When drafting policies that address issues of discrimination and harassment in schools, a whole-school policy that includes clear, definite guidelines on actions that are bias-motivated, including response protocols and implementation strategies, is essential (Arora, 1994; Cartwright, 1995; Sharp & Smith, 1991; Whitney & Smith, 1993). Language must also be clear and consistent and include specific protections against harassment, violence, and discrimination based on sexual orientation and gender identity or expression (Goldstein, Collins, & Halder, 2005).

Education A policy will not be effective unless those expected to enforce it are made aware of their obligations, and community members are informed of the

changes. Examples of such efforts include discussing the new policy in staff meetings, inviting a law expert to present a workshop on definitions of harassment and
the school's duty in preventing it, creating study circles within the staff to examine the new policy and discuss implementation strategies, publishing information
in school newsletters, Websites, and distributing brochures that include information
about the new policy.

Resources and support The school district needs to allocate resources like time,
money, and materials to ensure that these shifts in school climate can occur. Instead
of hiring a one-time invited speaker, some school boards have created full-time positions in order to ensure that they have the expertise and knowledge readily available
to support efforts in individual schools. In the state of Massachusetts (Perrotti &
Westheimer, 2001) and the Toronto District School Board, several positions were
created that were integral to the success of their programs, such as human sexuality program workers, equity department instructional leaders and student program
workers (Goldstein et al., 2005). The institutional support offered by these various
initiatives gives credibility and value to the daily efforts of individuals on the front
lines.

7.3.2 Teachers and Support Staff

Teachers and support staff, such as bus drivers, cafeteria personnel, and lunchroom
monitors, have the greatest opportunity to observe and intervene in incidents of
discrimination and harassment in schools. Teachers and support staff can focus
their development in the following areas: understanding of school policies, sharing
and practicing tools for intervening in incidents of discrimination and harassment,
and finding and using appropriate curricular materials and programs that are inclusive of gender and sexual diversity. These expectations mean that teachers and
support staff will need to attend workshops and courses, and take some responsibility for their own professional development in addition to participating in the
educational opportunities provided by the school administration. There are many
resources available for these pursuits, some of which are listed in the reference
list at the end of this chapter. Examples of curricular and extracurricular lessons
and activities are presented in detail in Chapter 4. Some examples that can address
some of the underlying issues of homophobia and heteronormativity include the
following:

(1) A campaign against name-calling that includes education about what words
    mean and why certain insults are inappropriate and discriminatory.
(2) Curricular inclusion of contributions by gays, lesbians, bisexuals, and trans-
    gender people to history, art, science, literature, politics, and sport.
(3) Providing inclusive and diverse information about sex, gender, and sexuality in
    biology, health, and sexual education classes.
(4) Conducting critical media literacy activities that analyze stereotypes related to
    heteronormativity, homophobia, sexism, and transphobia in popular culture.

Although teachers and support staff have a significant impact on school climate, without the participation of the student body, a true shift in culture and behavior cannot take place.

7.3.3 Students

Students comprise the largest percentage of a school community and are the trend-setters for what is valued in school. Without the support and investment of student leaders, there will continue to be student-only spaces where incidents of discrimination and harassment take place such as locker areas, washrooms, and areas in playgrounds and athletics fields. Schools that successfully engage student leaders, such as athletics team captains, student council members, peer mediators and others, can have a much broader and deeper impact on the lives of all students in school. Ways that this can be done include conducting summer leadership retreats, student discussion groups or weekend workshops that educate students about sexual diversity and solicit their help and support in challenging homophobia, heterosexism, and other forms of bias in the school. In addition to engaging prominent students in the school population, all students should be informed of the school's policies on harassment and discrimination by posting a code of conduct in each classroom, having students sign a behavior contract, and/or by having home-room discussions about the policy, what it means, and how it might affect them.

7.3.4 Families and Community Members

Finally, no school community is complete without the input and influence of families and community members. The parents' association and other community groups should be invited and encouraged to become actively involved in developing the school policy and educational strategies. By developing these partnerships early on, schools can anticipate any resistance or potential backlash and work through these issues before they grow into negative publicity for the school. To be a supportive and inclusive school, it is important to reach out to same-sex parented families to let them know that their input and involvement is welcomed. Gay and lesbian parents may stay closeted or separate from the school community if they have not been given any positive indicators that their family will be valued and included in that community. Most families are deeply invested in the education and development of their children and therefore should be included in such initiatives. Although there might be some resistance to addressing gender and sexual diversity in schools, by building strong ties with parent groups and other community organizations, schools can create a lasting network that will potentially expand their efforts to reduce such bias in the community at large.

Gender and sexual diversity are all around us. By ignoring it, schools cannot make the controversies surrounding it disappear. In many of the legal cases mentioned earlier, ignoring the issues exacerbated and escalated the problems. As educators who are responsible for supporting and teaching the next generation, it is our responsibility to create schools and classrooms that value and teach about the diversity that is already present in our communities. By unlearning the harmful messages from old stereotypes and misinformation, educators have the potential to create and teach more contemporary messages of equality, inclusiveness, and diversity.

7.4 Challenges and Solutions

Although there are many challenges to creating schools that value gender and sexual diversity, great progress has been made and this work must continue. The efforts of parents, teachers, administrators and community groups to effect change in their local schools and school districts are the reasons for the proliferation of gay–straight alliances in high schools across the United States and Canada. Grassroots mobilization and the building of local alliances have helped reform school policies and in-service teacher training programs. The leadership of youth confronting extreme instances of sexual and homophobic harassment in their schools has led to important legal precedents that have broad, long-term impacts. For every challenge that you can anticipate or have experienced, there are strong, wise, and passionate educators who have successfully navigated similar obstacles. Four key steps to take in working to address the challenges one might face in working to created schools that value gender and sexual diversity are

(1) Create coalitions
(2) Build foundations for long-term, sustainable change
(3) Identify priorities and strategies
(4) Sustain your spirit

   The rest of this chapter explores these topics and provides specific advice on how to successfully take each of these steps.

7.4.1 Create Coalitions

An important first step in working to create schools that value gender and sexual diversity is to identify and build relationships with key allies in your school and community. Before engaging in potentially controversial projects, developing the support and building on the wisdom of experienced teachers, administrators, and community groups is essential for long-term success. These allies and coalition members can provide much needed institutional knowledge, experience, insights, and personal and professional support. If you are a teacher, particularly if you are early in your career, it is very important to identify at least one administrator who is supportive of your efforts. This will allow you to understand any concerns that the administration might have and gives them the opportunity to provide you with support in case a controversy or complaint may arise.

In addition to keeping close contact with an ally in your school's administration and by creating a strong network of individuals and organizations who share your vision and goals, you not only gain from their knowledge and their networks, but you are also laying the foundation for long-term and sustainable changes. Building a coalition may seem to create unnecessary delays in taking steps to address these issues; however, it is an important step that can provide personal and professional support throughout the change process. Although it is difficult, it is important to be patient and continue working with others. If you forge ahead alone you may find yourself exhausted and out on a limb without any support. Additionally, although having an inspired and charismatic leader at the core of any coalition is valuable and helpful, it is important to share leadership and cultivate commitment and ownership in the goals of the coalition with others. Many good initiatives have folded when the driving force behind them moves or changes schools; so it is important to share responsibility and ownership of any change effort in order to ensure its long-term success.

7.4.2 Lay Foundations for Long-Term Change

Laying the foundation for long-term change is a second important step in ensuring that your efforts are sustainable. Creating this foundation requires patience as it can be a time-consuming process. For example, if you'd like to see tangible actions follow the addition of "sexual orientation and gender identity/expression" to school harassment and non-discrimination policies, you must work with that long-term solution in mind. One strategy is to quietly add the wording at the last minute of a rewriting of the policy to avoid a protracted public debate of the issue, and then once the policy has passed use that as leverage for adding an education/implementation program. Conversely, it may benefit your community to engage in a more extended debate and reformulation of policy language in order to build more support for the issue and the initiatives that are to follow. For those who are anxious to see immediate change, it can be quite a struggle to balance the need to build public support and a strong coalition along with the desire to see tangible progress toward the main projects of the coalition. Identifying priorities and strategies among members of the coalition can also be a lengthy and difficult process since members come to the process with different perspectives, leadership styles, and immediate needs. This brings us to the third item to consider when identifying challenges and solutions: identifying priorities and strategies.

7.4.3 Identify Priorities and Strategies

When working to transform school cultures, one must have a deep understanding of the realities and issues unique to each school community. Members of a coalition must be well informed about

(1) members of the school board and their political affiliations
(2) existing school and district policies
(3) current curricular guidelines and expectations,
(4) available local resources for presentations, workshops and in-service activities
     on gender and sexual diversity
(5) recent efforts and outcomes of related reform efforts in your state or province.

A working understanding of these issues will allow you and your allies to identify the priorities that are most pressing and relevant to your local community. There are a few helpful case studies available of local groups working to reform their school policies and how they were able to succeed in their efforts (see Faulkner & Lindsey, 2004; Goldstein et al., 2005; Macgillivray, 2004; Perrotti & Westheimer, 2001). These case studies offer in-depth road maps of the lengthy processes of implementing a local policy change and initiating a statewide educational initiative. These reports offer helpful strategies and insights about how to work creatively through obstacles as well as how to generate public support for a potentially "controversial" policy change. Finally, the most important element of engaging in work to transform school cultures is to sustain your spirit so you can engage in these projects in the long term.

7.4.4 Sustain Your Spirit

Sustaining your spirit can be a challenge if you are faced with resistance from colleagues, employers, community members and even family and friends. If you have made a decision to work to create schools that value gender and sexual diversity it probably means that you are deeply committed to and passionate about these issues. Most activists and educators who choose to work in the area of gender and sexual diversity do so out of necessity: to ensure the safety of a loved one or to protect one's current job. As you may already know, working against the current of established practices and institutional norms can be extremely time-consuming and emotionally draining. Therefore, it is important that you give yourself permission to take a break every now and then and allow yourself to make mistakes and let small issues slide.

In my first teaching job I was counseled to "pick my battles" when I was starting to advocate for issues related to gender equity and homophobia in my school community. I didn't like this advice since I thought that each of these "battles" was important and needed to be addressed. What I learned was that I was doing myself and my students a disservice by tackling every perceived injustice, and it reduced my credibility with my colleagues and administration. I had a hard time prioritizing, and strategizing and letting some issues move to the back burner. What I also learned, and was able to apply in another school, is that I was then able to conserve my energy and focus it more clearly on the issues that I thought would have more far-reaching and long-term impacts. Another way I learned to sustain my spirit was through connecting with like-minded individuals by attending conferences and social gatherings that allowed me to get ideas from others, as well as to feel understood, valued, and supported. Finding and creating these spaces for yourself is important if you want to ensure that you will not burn out and you will be able to continue engaging in such reform efforts beyond a short 1- or 2-year sprint. Lasting change takes time and during that time you need to be sure that you keep your own batteries fully charged so you can stay healthy, focused, and fulfilled as you face the daily challenges of supporting youth through grassroots activism and education reform.

7.5 Conclusion

Addressing issues of gender and sexual diversity in schools is challenging but important work. This book was written to provide current and future educators as well as committed youth workers a deeper and clearer understanding of the multiple interrelated issues that emerge in schools related to gender and sexual diversity. These issues touch very sensitive cultural nerves related to notions of relationships, identity, community, family, and religion. In order to more effectively work to create schools that value gender and sexual diversity, we must inform ourselves and take carefully planned and strategic steps. I hope that the information and resources provided in this book will provide you with the support and information you need to begin or continue working to make schools places where all students feel valued and included, where all families feel recognized and supported, and all professionals can fully express their whole selves. Schools will continue to be places where students, teachers, and families are hurt, isolated, and excluded from learning and fully engaging in their communities until all of these objectives are achieved.

Although the focus of this book has been on gender and sexual diversity it is important to acknowledge that there are many levels of diversity that impact individual's lives and experiences in schools: gender and sexuality are only two. When building coalitions and engaging in further education on diversity issues, it is important to recognize the multiple identities and oppressions that influence our experiences. Schools continue to marginalize individuals on the basis of race, ethnicity, religion, language, disability, and class to name just a few other variables. In order to apply the educational philosophies of democratic education, critical pedagogy, critical multiculturalism, feminist pedagogy, social justice education, anti-oppressive education, and queer pedagogy, these multiple factors must also be addressed. Please keep your mind open and your coalitions strong by working together to make schools better for all. I conclude this book with a list of resources to assist you on this journey. Best of luck and *bon courage!*

7.6 Resources

The following section provides a list of resources that may be helpful to educators looking to expand their own knowledge of these issues and/or to incorporate issues related to gender and sexual diversity in their classroom teaching. Each resource is given a cost rating (see below) since many of them are free or low in cost. I also provide a brief summary of the resource so you can more readily identify which will be of most help to you and your own school community.

Cost ratings

$ = $50 or less
$$ = $50–$150
$$$ = $150–500
$$$$ = $500 and above

7.6.1 School-Wide Interventions

7.6.1.1 Ally Week (Free)
www.glsen.org/allyweek

This event organized by the Gay, Lesbian, and Straight Education Network is held every October to end anti-LGBT bullying and harassment in K–12 schools by building ties with "allies." Allies are identified as people who advocate for the equality of a marginalized group, but do not identify as a member of that group. In the case of this event, most allies identify as heterosexual or normatively gendered. The goal of this event is to get students to sign an ally pledge to intervene in incidents of anti-LGBT bullying and harassment.

7.6.1.2 Challenge Day ($$$$)
www.challengeday.org

This non-profit community building initiative can be a valuable way to jumpstart anti-bullying and harassment work in a school. It can be somewhat costly for a school community as they require pre-program coaching for student leaders and staff as well as multiple days of workshops with the larger school community if you are over an hour from their base in Concord, CA. However, it has proven to be a powerful and healing experience that has positive impacts on the culture of the school as well as the students who participate. Some of the activities during the day explicitly address issues of systemic oppression including gender and sexual orientation. The goal of this event is "to build connection and empathy, and to fulfill our vision that every child lives in a world where they feel safe, loved, and celebrated."

7.6.1.3 Day of Silence (Free)
www.dayofsilence.org

This somewhat controversial event began in 1996 at the University of Virginia when a group of students chose to remain silent for one day to call attention to the anti-LGBT name-calling and harassment at their school. In 2007 over 5,000 middle and high schools registered to participate. There has been backlash in some communities against this event, but students and teachers who have participated indicate that it is a non-confrontational, yet empowering way to highlight these issues in a school community. This Website provides guidance and free resources to help student groups organize this event in their school community.

7.6.1.4 The International Day Against Homophobia (Free)
http://www.homophobiaday.org/

This annual educational campaign was started in 2003 in Quebec, Canada to increase public awareness about homophobia. This Website provides informational posters and publications for schools and other organizations to participate in the activities on May 17 and year round.

7.6.1.5 Mix It up at Lunch (Free)
http://www.tolerance.org/teens/lunch.jsp

This annual event encourages students to break out of their cliques and cross divisions in their school's social culture at lunchtime. Sponsored by the Southern Poverty Law Center's Teaching Tolerance program.

7.6.1.6 No Name Calling Week (Free/$$)
www.nonamecallingweek.org

Inspired by James Howe's novel *The Misfits*, this event has grown into a nation-wide phenomenon since its first organized instance in March of 2004. There are free downloadable resources on the Website, as well as a kit that can be purchased online. This is targeted toward students in Grades 5–8 and explicitly addresses biased forms of name-calling and harassment that happens between students, including homophobia. Many school-wide organizing ideas as well as classroom activities are available.

7.6.1.7 Olweus Bullying Prevention Program (Guide $$; Training $$$$)
http://www.clemson.edu/olweus/

This school-wide intervention kit provides all the information necessary to conduct a school-wide survey and interventions for a school community. This program offers school-, classroom-, and individual-level components for training and community involvement. They highly recommend using their trainers when implementing their program. Although it offers one of the most widely studied bullying intervention programs with a documented record of reducing incidents of overt bullying, its focus on behavioral interventions and lack of attention to issues of sex, gender, sexual orientation, and other forms of bias indicates that it may not be as effective in reducing forms of gendered harassment.

7.6.1.8 *Ugly Ducklings* (Free to Schools in Maine/$$)
www.uglyducklings.org

This film and educational kit was designed to promote dialogue around issues connected to teen suicide and homophobia. The film follows a group of young women at a summer retreat and allows the viewer to share their powerful emotional experiences as the participants learn and talk about these issues.

7.6.2 Staff Development

7.6.2.1 *Challenging Silence, Challenging Censorship* ($)
http://www.ctf-fce.ca/e/publications/ctf_publications.asp

This resource is a valuable guide for librarians as well as other educators interested in providing resources and support for GLBT youth, families, and their allies. It provides an annotated bibliography of books and materials for students of all ages.

7.6.2.2 *GLSEN Lunchbox* ($$)
www.glsenstore.org

This training toolkit provides many interactive activities, videos, and fact sheets on GLBT issues in schools. This kit is valuable for consultants, resource centers, and organizations that provide in-service training and support on issues related to sex, gender, and sexual orientation for educators. GLSEN also provides training institutes on using the toolkit effectively and developing facilitators' skills.

7.6.2.3 *It Takes a Team* (Free/$) Video and Resources
www.ittakesateam.org

This kit specifically addresses how gender and sexual orientation stereotypes can harm athletes, coaches, and the team environment. The kit includes a video, action guides, posters, stickers, and additional resources that can be helpful for coaches and athletes at the secondary and university level.

7.6.2.4 *It's Elementary: Talking About Gay Issues in Schools* ($$) Video & Discussion Guide
http://www.groundspark.org/films/elementary/

This now-classic documentary is one of the best teaching resources that models age-appropriate ways to talk about gay and lesbian issues with elementary age students. A particular strength of this film is that it has footage from actual classroom activities and discussions. It also does an excellent job including the experiences of students from different regions of the United States and of diverse ethnic and cultural backgrounds. A follow-up film, *Its STILL Elementary,* that follows up with students from the original film is now available as well.

7.6.2.5 *Just Call Me Kade* ($$) Video
http://cart.frameline.org/ProductDetails.asp?ProductCode=T526

This award-winning documentary traces the transition of an adolescent FTM (female-to-male) transgendered person. This resource provides a valuable first person narrative for those who are new to learning about transgender issues.

7.6.2.6 *Lessons Learned* ($)
http://www.ctf-fce.ca/e/publications/ctf_publications.asp

This short publication put out by the Canadian Teachers' Federation provides a brief introduction to terminology and studies as well as collection of stories and experiences from educators working in anti-homophobia education to better understand the cultural and political contexts for addressing GLBT issues in Canadian schools.

7.6.2.7 *Seeking Educational Equity and Diversity–SEED* ($$$$)
http://www.wcwonline.org/?option=com_content&task=view &id=893&Itemid=54

The National SEED Project on Inclusive Curriculum, a staff-development equity project for educators, is in its 22nd year of establishing teacher-led faculty development seminars in public and private schools throughout the United States and in English-speaking international schools. A week-long SEED summer New Leaders' Workshop prepares school teachers to hold year-long reading groups with other teachers to discuss making school climates and curricula more gender-fair and multiculturally equitable.

7.6.2.8 *Straitlaced: How Gender's Got Us All Tied Up!* ($$) Video
http://groundspark.org/our-films-and-campaigns/straightlaced

This film interviews 50 teens from all backgrounds and explores how the heteronormative ideals of masculinity and femininity impact everyone. Presented by the filmmakers who made *It's Elementary* and *That's a Family*, this film is a valuable instructional tool for any school staff that is looking to address how gender roles play out in their own school communities. This can also be effectively used with older secondary school students.

7.6.2.9 *Teaching Respect for All* ($) Video
www.glsenstore.org

This training video captures a compelling talk given to an audience of teachers, administrators, and counselors by GLSEN Executive Director, author, and former high school teacher, Kevin Jennings. He is a dynamic and compelling speaker and this video captures the key points for educators to understand when addressing homophobia and GLBT issues in schools.

7.6.3 K–12 Classroom

7.6.3.1 *Dealing With Differences* ($) Video & Teacher Guide
www.glsenstore.org

This lesson kit is available to order from GLSEN and provides a 20-min video and discussion guides for teachers to introduce conversations about respect and anti-LGBT harassment in the secondary classroom (grades 7–12).

7.6.3.2 Gender Doesn't Limit You! (Free)
http://www.tolerance.org/teach/activities/activity.jsp?ar=841
&ttnewsletter=ttnewsgen-091307

This series of six lesson plans combines information on reducing gender stereotypes in early grades (K–4) with bullying intervention strategies. Researchers working on this project found that this curriculum successfully increased students' willingness to take a stand to counteract bullying.

7.6.3.3 GLSEN (Free/$) Lesson Plans and Resource Lists
http://www.glsen.org/cgi-bin/iowa/all/library/curriculum.html

This non-profit organization has a Website that is full of free downloadable lesson plans (K–12) and reading lists (sorted by age) to assist teachers interested in integrating information about sex, gender, and sexual orientation as well as related forms of diversity education into their classes.

7.6.3.4 *Let's Get Real!* ($$) Video and Curriculum Guide
http://www.groundspark.org/films/letsgetreal/index.html

This film addresses multiple forms of bias and harassment that happens in schools. It provides first-hand narratives from students who have been targeted as well as from students who have taken a stand on behalf of others. The wide variety of issues covered in this film provides a valuable starting point for talking about bias and harassment with students in grades 6–12.

7.6.3.5 Media Awareness Network (Free) Lesson Plans and Resources
www.media-awareness.ca

This bilingual site (French and English) provides a rich variety of lessons on gender and stereotypes using media texts. Teachers can search by grade level (K–12) or topic for classroom activities and resources.

7.6.3.6 *Tough Guise* ($$) Video
http://www.mediaed.org/

This educational video is geared toward high school students to help them examine the relationships between popular culture images and the construction of masculinity. This entertaining and well-researched film provides an engaging approach to understanding how gender and violence are related and the pressure on boys to put on a "tough guise." The Media Education Foundation has a wealth of other resources on gender, sexual orientation, and the media on their Website.

7.6.3.7 *Welcoming Schools* (Free)
http://www.hrc.org/welcomingschools/

This curriculum guide for K–5 schools was developed by the *Human Rights Campaign* to help provide resources to elementary schools that are actively working to be more inclusive of all forms of diversity in their communities. This resource goes beyond offering lesson plans and includes a checklist to evaluate the climate of a school community as well as sample policy wording. It is an excellent comprehensive resource for elementary schools that addresses multiple layers of diversity and prominently includes BGLQT topics and concerns.

References

Arora, C. M. J. (1994). Is there any point in trying to reduce bullying in secondary schools? A Two Year Follow-up of a Whole-School Anti-Bullying Policy in One School. *Educational Psychology in Practice, 10*(3), 155–162.

Britzman, D. (2000). Precocious Education. In S. Talburt & S. Steinberg (Eds.), *Thinking Queer: Sexuality, culture, and education* (pp. 33–60). New York: Peter Lang.

Cartwright, N. (1995). Combating bullying in a secondary school in the United Kingdom. *Journal for a Just and Caring Education, 1*(3), 345–353.

Faulkner, A. O., & Lindsey, A. (2004). Grassroots meet homophobia: A Rocky mountain success story. *Journal of Gay and Lesbian Social Services: Issues in Practice, Policy, & Research, 16*(3–4).

Goldstein, T., Collins, A., & Halder, M. (2005). *Challenging Homophobia and Heterosexism in elementary and high schools: A research report to the Toronto District school board*. Toronto, ON: Ontario Instituted for Studies in Education of the University of Toronto.

Goodenow, C., Szalacha, L., & Westhimer, K. (2006). School support groups, other school factors, and the safety of sexual minority adolescents. *Psychology in the Schools, 43*(5), 573–589.

Greytak, E., & Kosciw, J. (2008). *Leadership for school safety: The Principal's perspective on school climate for lesbian, gay, bisexual, and transgender students and families*. Paper presented at The Annual Meeting of the American Educational Research Association.

Kosciw, J., Diaz, E., & Gretytak, E. (2008). *2007 National school climate survey: The experiences of lesbian, gay, bisexual, and transgender youth in our nation's schools*. New York: GLSEN.

Macgillivray, I. K. (2004). Gay rights and school policy: A case study in community factors that facilitate or impede educational change. *International Journal of Qualitative Studies in Education, 17*(3), 347–370.

Meyer, E. J. (2008a). Gendered harassment in secondary schools: Understanding teachers' (non)interventions. *Gender & Education, 20*(6), 555–572.

138   7 Transforming School Cultures

Meyer, E. J. (2008b). Who we are matters: Exploring teacher identities through found poetry. *LEARNing Landscapes, 1*(3), 195–210.

Meyer, E. J. (2009). *Gender, bullying, and harassment: Strategies to end sexism and homophobia in schools.* New York: Teachers College Press.

Perrotti, J., & Westheimer, K. (2001). *When the drama club is not enough: Lessons from the safe schools program for Gay and Lesbian students.* Boston, MA: Beacon Press.

Sharp, S., & Smith, P. K. (1991). Bullying in UK schools: The DES sheffield bullying project. *Early Child Development and Care, 77*, 47–55.

Stader, D. L., & Graca, T. J. (2007). School culture and sexual minority teachers in the United States. *Journal of Education and Human Development, 1*(2).

Thonemann, A. (1999, December 1). *Enabling and disabling conditions for teaching against homophobia.* Paper presented at the Australian Association for Research in Education Conference, Melbourne, Australia.

Whitney, I., & Smith, P. K. (1993). A survey of the nature and extent of bullying in junior/middle and secondary schools. *Educational Research, 35*(1), 3–25.

Additional Reading

Bochenek, M., & Brown, A. W. (2001). *Hatred in the hallways: Violence and discrimination against lesbian, gay, bisexual, and transgender students in U.S. schools*: Human Rights Watch.
This important study summarizes the often painful and difficult experiences of GLBT students in schools around the United States and provides a concise summary of legal protections that exist for GLBT students in U.S. schools.

Bornstein, K. (1998). *My gender workbook.* New York: Routledge.
This "workbook" was written by a transgender performer and activists and includes reflective activities on gender and society and is written in an engaging and accessible voice. It is a great introduction for anyone learning about how gender shapes us and our relationships with others.

Brown, L. M. (2003). *Girlfighting: Betrayal and rejection among girls.* New York: New York University Press.
This book by respected gender scholar Lyn Mikel Brown synthesizes the voices of over 400 interviews with girls in the United States and provides an insightful analysis of the gender issues involved in relationships among girls.

Duncan, N. (1999). *Sexual bullying: Gender conflict and pupil culture in secondary schools.* London: Routledge.
This book summarizes the findings of an ethnographic study of a secondary school in England and provides detailed analyses of the role of gender, sex, and sexual orientation in influencing peer relations in the school community.

Killoran, I., & Jimenez, K. P. (Eds.). (2007). *"Unleashing the unpopular": Talking about sexual orientation and gender diversity in education.* Olney, MD: Association for Childhood Education International.
This is an edited collection of stories from students, teachers, and researchers about their experiences with gender and sexual diversity in their lives and schools.

Kissen, R. (Ed.). (2002). *Getting ready for Benjamin: Preparing teachers for sexual diversity in the classroom.* Oxford: Rowman Littlefield.
This edited collection includes a series of essays by teachers and teacher educators on the issues of pre-service teacher education. This is a valuable text as it provides first-person narratives about the personal struggles as well and the pedagogical choices made when working to teach about sexual diversity in teacher education programs.

Lipkin, A. (1999). *Understanding homosexuality, changing schools.* Boulder, CO: Westview Press.

This is one of the earliest and most comprehensive texts that address issues related to homophobia and schools. Lipkin's book is detailed and addresses a wide variety of issues including: history, identity, counseling, families, and curriculum. Although some of its information is now somewhat dated, it is still an invaluable reference.

Mac an Ghaill, M. (1995). *The making of men: Masculinities, sexualities, and schooling.* Philadelphia, PA: Open University Press.

This is one of the first books that explore the connections between masculinity, homophobia, bullying and social relations in school. A very rich and nuanced analysis of varying forms of masculinity in school.

Macgillivray, I. K. (2007). *Gay-straight alliances: A handbook for students, educators, and parents.* New York: Harrington Park Press.

A concise and easy-to-read guide that provides practical advice and detailed resources for students, teachers, administrators, and parents engaged in creating or working with Gay–Straight Alliances.

Meyer, E. (2009). *Gender, bullying, and harassment: Strategies to end sexism and homophobia in schools.* New York: Teachers College Press.

This book specifically addresses issues of bullying, harassment, and school violence that are related to homophobia, sexism and transphobia. It provides an overview of my research project and a checklist of steps to take to reduce gendered harassment in schools.

Pascoe, C.J. (2007) *Dude you're a fag: Masculinity and sexuality in high school.* University of California Press.

This book provides an incisive view of how masculinity and sexualities are regulated and negotiated based on an in-depth study in one California high school.

Perrotti, J., & Westheimer, K. (2001). *When the drama club is not enough: Lessons from the safe schools program for Gay and Lesbian students.* Boston, MA: Beacon Press.

This is a practical and informative guide based on the work and experiences of educators working in Massachusetts with the first statewide program aimed at supporting GLBT youth in schools.

Steinberg, S. (Ed.). (2009). *Diversity and multiculturalism: A reader.* New York: Peter Lang.

This is one of the few texts on diversity and multiculturalism in education that has several chapters that address issues of gender and sexual diversity. I highly recommend this text for use in courses that deal with a wide variety of diversity issues.

Appendix: Glossary of Terms

Asexual   A sexual orientation for a person who does not feel sexual attraction or experience a desire for sexual contact.

BGLQT   Abbreviation for bisexual, gay, lesbian, queer, questioning, two-spirit, transsexual, and transgender people. You may also see it written as GLBT, LGBT, LGBQ, depending on the author and the participants in the study or document cited.

Bisexual   A sexual orientation for a person who is attracted to some members of both sexes to varying degrees. The prefix "bi" indicates the belief that there are only two sexes. See also: omnisexual,pansexual

Bullying   A student is being bullied or victimized when he or she is exposed, repeatedly and over time, to negative actions on the part of one or more other students...it is a negative action when someone intentionally inflicts, or attempts to inflict, injury or discomfort on another...Negative actions can be carried out by words (verbally), for instance, by threatening, taunting, teasing and calling names. It is a negative action when somebody hits, pushes, kicks, pinches or restrains another – by physical contact. It is also possible to carry out negative actions without the use of words or physical contact, such as by making faces or dirty gestures, intentionally excluding someone from a group, or refusing to comply with another person's wishes (Olweus, 1993, p. 9).

Cisgender   This term is borrowed from chemistry and used to describe individuals whose gender identity and expression aligns with social expectations for their sex assigned at birth. It is used to describe people who do not identify as transgender.

Compulsory heterosexuality   The theory advanced by poet and lesbian feminist Adrienne Rich that asserts that women are coerced by social structures to engage in heterosexual relationships with men. She argues that heterosexuality is a political institution, not just a naturally occurring phenomenon, and is a central feature of patriarchy (Rich, 1978/1993).

Discourse   Linguistic practices that shape social relations and cultural beliefs. Based in the work of French philosopher, Michel Foucault, it is considered to be the institutionalized way of thinking as established by how and what words are used in certain contexts (see also Jaworski & Coupland, 1999).

E.J. Meyer, *Gender and Sexual Diversity in Schools*, Explorations of Educational Purpose 10, DOI 10.1007/978-90-481-8559-7, © Springer Science+Business Media B.V. 2010

Disorder of Sex Development or DSD   is a general term used for a variety of conditions in which a person is born with a reproductive or sexual anatomy that doesn't seem to fit the typical definitions of female or male. For example, a person might be born appearing to be female on the outside, but having mostly male-typical anatomy on the inside. Or a person may be born with genitals that seem to be in between the usual male and female types. See also: intersex (ISNA, n.d.).

Euroheteropatriarchy   A term advanced by Francisco Valdez that provides a shorthand term for "the interlocking operation of dominant forms racism, ethno-centrism, androcentrism, and heterocentrism – all of which operate in tandem in the United States and beyond it to produce identity hierarchies that subordinate people of color, women, and sexual minorities in different yet similar and familiar ways" (Valdez, 2002, p. 404).

GLBT   Abbreviation for gay, lesbian, bisexual, two-spirit, transsexual, and transgender people.

Gay   The preferred term for a person who engages in same-sex relationships and identifies as a member of this community. It is preferred above the term "homosexual" as homosexual has scientific meanings that apply specifically to same-sex behaviors and does not consider a person's identities and relationships. "Gay" can refer to both men and women, although many women prefer the term lesbian.

Gender   A term used to describe those characteristics of women and men that are socially constructed, in contrast to those that are legally and biologically determined, sex. People are assigned a sex at birth, but learn to act like girls and boys who grow into women and men. They are taught what the appropriate behaviors, attitudes, roles and activities are for them, and how they should relate to other people. These learned attributes are what make up gender identity and expression as well as determine gender roles.

Gender expression   How one chooses to dress, walk, talk, and accessorize that expresses one's gender identity. Related terms include gender role performance and gender presentation.

Gender non-conformity   When a person's gender expression varies from that which is traditionally expected for a person of that sex. For example, when a male shows an interest in dance or fashion, or when a female enjoys rough and aggressive sports and activities. Related terms include gender atypical, gender-variant and gender non-normativity.

Gendered harassment   Any unwanted behavior that polices and reinforces the traditional notions of heterosexual masculinity and heterosexual femininity and includes (hetero)sexual harassment, homophobic harassment, and harassment for gender non-conformity (Meyer, 2006).

Gender identity   Refers to an individuals' innate sense of self as a man, woman, transgender, genderqueer, or other identification. This is often shaped by one's sex assigned at birth and the gender in which they are raised. It may change over time and may not fit in the traditional dichotomous gender categories of man/woman.

Genderqueer   A relatively new term used to describe an individual whose gender identity or expression extends beyond the binary of man or woman and actively challenges the heteronormative gender binary system. Individuals who identify as genderqueer may use a wide variety of labels such as androgyne, genderfluid, gender-gifted, gender outlaw, and intergender.

Harassment   Biased behaviors that have a negative impact on the target or the environment (Land, 2003). They may be intentional or unintentional.

Harassment for Gender Non-conformity   Any unwanted behavior that targets a person's perceived masculinity or femininity. Also referred to as transphobic harassment.

Hegemonic masculinity   From a theory advanced by R. Connell, it is the form of masculinity that occupies a dominant and privileged position in a given pattern of gender relations. In Western cultures this often defined by claims to authority (often through aggression, physical strength, dominance, institutional power), and heterosexuality, but is subject to change if social relations shift (Connell, 1995).

Homophobia   Fear or hatred of those assumed to be BGLQT and anything connected to their culture; when a person fears homosexuality, either in other people or within themselves. Homophobia can be attitudes or behaviors that range from mild discomfort to verbally abusive or physically violent acts.

Homophobic harassment   See sexual orientation harassment.

Heteronormativity   A term coined in 1991 by Michael Warner to describe a system of behaviors and social expectations that are built around the belief that everyone is or should be heterosexual and that all relationships and families follow this model (Warner, 1991). See also: Compulsory Heterosexuality, Heterosexism, and Heterosexual Matrix.

Heterosexism   A bias towards heterosexuality that denigrates and devalues BGL people. Also, the presumption that heterosexuality is superior to homosexuality or, prejudice, bias or discrimination based on these things.

(Hetero)sexual harassment   Any unwanted behavior that has a sexual or gender component and is enacted within the matrix of heterosexual relations. It includes two main types of harassment: quid pro quo and hostile environment. Quid pro quo harassment is an explicit offer of an exchange such as, "I will give you a better grade if you do a sexual favor for me." Hostile environment harassment is more common in schools and includes any behavior that acts to create a hostile environment such as graffiti, jokes, comments, gestures, looks, and unwanted touching.

Heterosexual Matrix   A concept advanced by gender theorist Judith Butler that builds on Adrienne Rich's notion of compulsory heterosexuality. Butler states that all gender relations are built within the boundaries of the "oppositionally and hierarchically defined … compulsory practice of heterosexuality" (Butler, 1990, p. 194).

Intersex is a general term used for a variety of cases in which a person is born with a reproductive or sexual anatomy that doesn't seem to fit the typical definitions of female or male. For example, a person might be born appearing to be female on the outside, but having mostly male-typical anatomy on the inside. Or a person may be born with genitals that seem to be in between the usual male and female types. Although this was the preferred term for some time, some advocates now prefer the term Disorder of Sex Development or DSD (ISNA, n.d.).

Lesbian The preferred term for a woman who engages in same-sex relationships and identifies as a member of this community. It is preferred above the term "homosexual" as it has scientific meanings that apply specifically to same-sex behaviors and does not consider a person's identities and relationships.

Omnisexual A person who is attracted to some members of any sex to varying degrees. The prefix "omni" from the Latin for all, indicates the belief that there are many sexes.

Pansexual A person who is attracted to some members of all sexes to varying degrees. The prefix "pan" from the Greek for all, indicates the belief that there are many sexes.

Patriarchy The basic definition of a patriarchy is a society that is governed and controlled by men. Feminist theorists have used this term to explain the current gender system that gives males access to power and social privileges and in turn marginalizes and oppresses people of all other genders. See also: heterosexism, sexism

Sex A medico-legal category that is assigned at birth based on certain biological characteristics that vary by region. Such characteristics may include a child's chromosomes, gonadal tissue, hormone levels, and external genitalia. Sexual dimorphism is often thought to be a scientific reality, whereas individuals who are intersex point to a multiplicity of sexes in the human population. This is different from gender which is socio-cultural as noted above.

Sexism The belief or attitude that women are inferior to men, also related to misogyny. This results in oppression and discrimination against women in patriarchal societies.

Sexual harassment (see Heterosexual harassment)

Sexual orientation This term describes the genders and sexes towards which a person is emotionally, physically, romantically and erotically attracted to such as homosexual, bisexual, omnisexual, heterosexual, and asexual and is informed by innate sexual attraction. In all instances, use this term instead of sexual preference or other misleading terminology. Trans and gender-variant people may identify with any sexual orientation, and their sexual orientation may or may not change before, during, or after transition.

Sexual Orientation harassment   Any unwanted behavior that insults or harms gays, lesbians, and bisexuals, or uses anti-GLB insults to insult or harm another person. May be targeted at GLB people or non-GLB people. See also : Homophobic harassment

Social Construct   This concept emerged from sociology and psychology to describe concepts and terms that exist because a society or culture has collectively decided to agree that it exists. Some examples include money, citizenship, race and gender.

Transgender   An umbrella term, like "trans" for individuals who blur the lines of traditional gender expression. Usually including transsexual and sometimes also including cross dressers. These individuals may or may not choose to change physical characteristics of their bodies or legally change their sex.

Transsexual   is a term used to describe a person who lives in a gender that is different from the sex they were assigned at birth. Many transsexual people opt to undergo physical transformations such as surgery and hormone therapy so that their bodies more closely align with social norms for their gender identities. Although it is categorized as one type of gender identity disorder by the American Psychological Association's Diagnostic and Statistical Manual, many advocates have worked to remove this designation from the DSM in order to reduce the stigma and association with mental illness often attached to individuals who are transsexual.

Transphobia   The irrational fear and hatred of all individuals who transgress, violate, or blur the dominant gender categories in a given society. Transphobic attitudes can lead to discrimination, violence and oppression against the gay, lesbian, bisexual, trans, and intersex communities as well as gender non-conforming individuals.

Transphobic harassment   see Harassment for gender non-conformity

Two-spirit   is a term used to describe members of First Nations, Native American, and Métis communities who also identify as bisexual, gay, lesbian, or transgender. This term is an attempt at translating concepts and terms from various North American aboriginal cultures that had spiritual leaders and community members who were respected and appreciated for their abilities to understand and express qualities of both men and women. Individuals who use this term often use it to embrace their cultural identities as First Nations or Native people as well as their BGLTQ identities.

Verbal harassment   Persistent and repeated negative behaviors that are unwanted and verbal in nature such as name-calling, insults, sexual jokes, and graffiti. As with other forms of harassment it may be intentional or unintentional.

References

Butler, J. (1990). *Gender trouble*. New York: Routledge Falmer.

Connell, R. W. (1995). *Masculinities*. Sydney: Allen and Unwin.

ISNA. (n.d.). What is intersex? Retrieved August 19, 2009, from http://www.isna.org/faq/what_is_intersex

Jaworski, A., & Coupland, N. (1999). Introduction: Perspectives on discourse analysis. In A. Jaworski & N. Coupland (Eds.), *The discourse reader* (pp. 1–44). London: Routledge.

Land, D. (2003). Teasing apart secondary students' conceptualizations of peer teasing, bullying and sexual harassment *School Psychology International, 24*(2), 147–165.

Meyer, E. J. (2006). Gendered harassment in North America: School-based interventions for reducing homophobia and heterosexism. In C. Mitchell & F. Leach (Eds.), *Combating gender violence in and around Schools* (pp. 43–50). Stoke on Trent, UK: Trentham Books.

Olweus, D. (1993). *Bullying at school: What we know and what we can do*. Oxford: Blackwell Publishing.

Rich, A. (1978/1993). Compulsory heterosexuality and lesbian existence. In H. Abelove, D. Halperin, & M. A. Barale (Eds.), *The lesbian and gay studies reader* (pp. 227–254). New York: Routledge.

Valdez, F. (2002). Outsider scholars, critical race theory, and "outcrit" perspectivity: Postsubordination vision as jurisprudential method. In F. Valdez, J. M. Culp & A. P. Harris (Eds.), *Crossroads, directions, and a new critical race theory* (pp. 399–409). Philadelphia: Temple University Press.

Warner, M. (1991). Introduction: Fear of a queer planet. *Social Text, 29*, 3–17.

Author Index

Subject Index

CPSIA information can be obtained at www.ICGtesting.com
Printed in the USA
BVOW06s1413010916

460870BV00006B/38/P